TUSCAN COOKERY

BY ELISABETTA PIAZZESI

BONECHI

How to read the Cards

DIFFICULTY	FLAVOUR	NUTRITIONAL VALUE
● Simple	● Mild	● Low
●● Moderate	●● Moderately spicy	●● Medium
●●● Difficult	●●● Spicy	●●● High

Preparation and cooking times are shown in hours (h) and minutes (e. g. 30′ is 30 minutes).

Project: Casa Editrice Bonechi
Series editor: Alberto Andreini
Coordination: Paolo Piazzesi
Graphic design and make-up: Andrea Agnorelli
Cover: Maria Rosanna Malagrinò
Editing: Rina Bucci

Translation: Stephanie Johnson

Chef: Elisabetta Piazzesi
Dietician: Dr. John Luke Hili

The photographs of the food are the property of the Casa Editrice Bonechi Archives and were taken by Dario Grimoldi *and* Andrea Fantauzzo *(pages 11, 15, 29, 33, 35, 40, 44, 46, 49, 54-55, 57, 58-59, 64, 68, 69, 76-77, 78, 79, 80, 81, 82, 87, 94, 101, 102-103, 104, 108, 114, 118, 120)*

The landscape photographs are the property of the Casa Editrice Bonechi Archives and were taken by Genni Cappelli, R. Cecconi, Stefano Cellai, Luca Del Pia, Paolo Giambone, Mario Lari, M.S.A., Andrea Pistolesi, Aldo Umicini. *Pages 6, 22, 47, 50, 55, 76:* courtesy of Francesco Giannoni.

For the photographs with no identified source, the Publisher would appreciate any information so as to integrate reprinted editions.

E-mail : bonechi@bonechi.it *Internet :* www.bonechi.it

Printed in Italy by Centro Stampa Editoriale Bonechi.

ISBN 88-476-0780-9

* * *

PREFACE

Florence, Tuscany - my ancient, illustrious hometown and my charming, austere land, with its landscape moulded by Man around its natural beauty. Here we have the azure sea, there the hills and mountains with their green slopes gurgling with streams and dotted with villages... and the countryside, the meadows, the wheat which gives us our unsalted bread, an unrepeatable miracle of simplicity. This is what our table fare is: it expresses modesty, wisdom and instinctive good taste. In order to appreciate that so much vitality is the consequence of authenticity, you only need linger a moment to reflect on the recipes, their style and daily application in the kitchen, and their ability to pass on the original spirit in its entirety, but at the same time adapt to changing habits and needs. And, to appreciate the ingeniousness, it is enough to contemplate how little is needed to prepare dishes fit for a king.

My cooking is born of tradition, recuperating its high cultural and gastronomic level, the aesthetical rigour and respect for things - to be handled wisely and simply, not violating them. You will not find here sauces swamping the dishes, neither are there indigestible, greasy dressings. Olive oil finds its legitimate place as a natural dressing, exalting flavours without blunting them, enriching even the humblest dish. The flavour of our cuisine is precisely this: much more than a gastronomic canon, it is a style of life.

Cooking is to breathe life into ingredients and model the elements which make up our fare. We cook not just in order to survive, but to afford us joy and pride in our meals. It is not just the gastronomic values which count, or a well turned out dish, or the appeasement of taste and the eye. Cooking is a civilised, cultured way to communicate. As far as Florentine and Tuscan cuisine is concerned, it also communicates grace and elegance.

All the recipes that you will find here have been tried out, step after step, especially for this book, which is my husband Pedro's as much as mine. The comments are intended to introduce variants, offer suggestions for preparing and cooking the dishes, and also to indicate when and how much the process differs from orthodox tradition... in order to better or simplify it, of course. Salt and pepper are not given in the list of ingredients, as their use goes without saying, just as you need water to cook the pasta or boil the vegetables. Listing them would be a waste of time and space (though indications are given in the recipe when the seasoning is to be added - preferably in moderation. If necessary, salt is present only in the list of ingredients for cakes and biscuits, where its use is not taken for granted. My advice is to read through the list of ingredients (also noted is the time needed for the preparation and cooking of the dish, with indications as to the level of difficulty and the intensity of flavour - whether more or less pronounced - together with the dietetical value), then to read each stage of the recipe carefully before starting out. As well as to my children, this book is dedicated to those who like to enjoy themselves in company around the dinner table.

NOTES FROM THE DIETICIAN

The so-called Mediterranean diet actually turns out to be "the island that is not". While its various traditional aspects are represented, its dictates are never entirely followed through by any of the people inhabiting the Mediterranean basin. That having been stated, we may add that the Tuscan cuisine sums up many of the characteristics of the Mediterranean diet.

For what reasons? This is, above all, the cuisine of the people, with simple ingredients, often using up left-overs. The socio-economic progress of the last fifty years has meant that we have forgotten this component and have made gastronomy richer in proteins and fats than it originally used to be.

Another aspect going unheeded is the balance between nutrients, actually the identity card of Mediterranean cuisine. Preference goes to carbohydrates (55-60%), especially the complex ones we get from cereals and their derivatives. Fats (30%) and proteins (20%) are represented to a correct degree. A further aspect is the appreciable presence of dietary fibre offered in healthy side dishes of vegetables and pulses. Finally, the use of the right proportion of extra virgin olive oil as the principle source of fat, especially oleic fatty acid which is monounsaturated - at least 50% of the fat total - an excellent foil against arteriosclerosis.

We conclude with wine, which in Tuscan cooking is much more than a mere complement. The history of the Tuscan hills is permeated with it just like the arteries of a gourmet, perhaps "oiled" by the wine itself (if consumed in modest quantities).

Index of Recipes

STARTERS AND SAUCES

PASTA, SOUP AND RICE DISHES

MEAT AND GAME

FISH AND SHELLFISH

OMELETTES

VEGETABLE DISHES

DESSERTS, CAKES AND PASTRIES

STARTERS AND SAUCES

1

Aringa sott'olio

Herrings in oil

2 salted herrings
2 carrots
1 head of celery
a few small, pickling onions
olive oil
chilli pepper

Servings: 4	
Preparation time: 20'+24h	
Difficulty: ●	
Flavour: ●●●	
Kcal (per serving): 233	
Proteins (per serving): 8	
Fats (per serving): 20	
Nutritional value: ●●●	

For serving in oil, herrings must not be smoked and should preferably be females with their roes, not males.
Bone the fish and rinse under running water. In a deep serving dish, lay the fillets on a bed of carrots, celery and fresh onions, all finely chopped.
Cover with olive oil and add one or two dried chilli peppers.
Leave to stand a while, a whole day even, before relishing them with white Tuscan bread.

A personal touch to a traditional dish? Boil some rather large potatoes. Allow to cool and cut into big, round slices. Cut up the herrings into small pieces (not too small) and simply serve on the potato rounds.

CARCIOFI SOTT'OLIO

Artichoke preserved in oil

10 small globe artichokes (morellini, if available)
1 l / 1$^3/_4$ pt / 4$^1/_2$ cups white wine
60ml / 2 fl oz / $^1/_4$ cup red wine vinegar
2 lemons
10 bay leaves
whole black pepper
olive oil

Servings: 4
Preparation time: 20'+24h
Cooking time: 15'
Difficulty: ●
Flavour: ●●
Kcal (per serving): 364
Proteins (per serving): 0
Fats (per serving): 20
Nutritional value: ●●●

Carefully clean the artichokes, trim the tops and emerge in a saucepan containing water and a squeeze of lemon. Put the saucepan on the heat, adding the white wine, vinegar, 2 bay leaves and 10 black peppercorns.

When cooked, the artichokes must still be crisp. Drain well, leaving them to dry upside-down on a tea towel, for a whole day if necessary. Put them in jars, alternating them with the bay leaves and a few peppercorns. Cover with good-quality olive oil and close the jars tightly. In this final phase, a chilli pepper or a pinch (and I mean just a pinch) of fennel seed can be added to your liking.

Morellini artichokes are purple in colour. They are one of my favourites for lending flavour to a nice rice salad, or for giving the finishing touch to a cold side-plate.

CIPOLLE IN AGRODOLCE

Sweet-sour onions

1kg / $2^1/4$ lb red-skinned onions
125ml / 4 fl oz / $^1/2$ cup red wine vinegar
3 tablespoons olive oil
1 tablespoon sugar
pinch of salt

Servings: 4-6
Preparation time: 10′
Cooking time: 3h 10′
Difficulty: ●
Flavour: ●●
Kcal (per serving): 147
Proteins (per serving): 2
Fats (per serving): 10
Nutritional value: ●●

We all immediately think of the commonplace white, cocktail onions commercialised on television and we are a little disconcerted when a plate piled high with a dark and mysterious mixture is put before us. Just try them and in this dish you will savour all the patience, experience and simplicity of Tuscan cuisine. Here we go again, talking about patience and time... A particular touch can be lent by eating them with fresh ricotta, ewe's milk cottage cheese: an unusual combination to dazzle and delight your guests.

Cut the onions into segments and blanche for a few minutes (in a pressure cooker, if preferred), until all the juices have run out.
Place in a pan (traditionally, you carry on with the same one as before), add all the other ingredients together in one fell swoop, put over a low flame... and wait. While waiting, frequently stir the mixture, and, little by little, it will change consistency and colour.
Three hours are necessary for good results (much, of course, also depends on the type of onion).

CROSTINI CON I FEGATINI

Chicken livers on toast

Trim the livers carefully, removing all traces of gall bladder. Rinse under the tap and leave to drain. Slice the onion finely and sauté in a pan with 2 tablespoons olive oil. When it begins to become translucent, add the livers. While cooking, gradually sprinkle in the vinsanto and season with salt and pepper. Cook over medium heat for half-an-hour. Finally add the capers, squeezed of all their vinegar. Chop up the sauce or, better still, pass through the mincing machine. Toast some slices of bread and sprinkle with just a little stock. Spread a portion of the mixture on each slice and serve. This is also good eaten cold.

300g / 11 oz chicken livers
a little stock
1 red-skinned onion
60ml / 2 fl oz / 4 tbsp vinsanto (or sherry)
50g / 2 oz / 1/4 cup capers
slices of white bread
olive oil

Servings: 4
Preparation time: 20′
Cooking time: 35′
Difficulty: ●●
Flavour: ●●
Kcal (per serving): 561
Proteins (per serving): 26
Fats (per serving): 14
Nutritional value: ●●●

CROSTINI COL VINSANTO

Vinsanto canapés

300g / 11 oz chicken livers
2 garlicky sausages
1 onion
sprig of rosemary
$^1/_2$ l / 1 pt / 2$^1/_4$ cups vinsanto (or medium-dry sherry)
slices of baguette-type bread
olive oil

Servings: 4
Preparation time: 15'
Cooking time: 45'
Difficulty: ●●
Flavour: ●●
Kcal (per serving): 912
Proteins (per serving): 35
Fats (per serving): 33
Nutritional value: ●●●

Slice the bread into many rounds to be dipped into the vinsanto. Place the slices on a serving dish. Sauté the chopped onion in a pan with a trickle of oil. Crumble the sausages in your hands and add to the onion when it is half cooked, keeping the pan over low heat for a quarter-hour. Rinse the livers carefully under the tap and add to the pan, together with the other ingredients. Continue cooking for half-an-hour over gentle heat, seasoning with salt, pepper and the sprig of rosemary. Discard the herb and put everything through the grinder. Serve the mixture on the bread rounds and offer to your family or guests.

Allow me to suggest, for a change, that this preparation does not need Tuscan bread, but rather the French baguette type, round in shape, with a softer texture to it. Vinsanto can be found behind every threshold in Tuscany, and, to borrow an old Italian adage, it is like parsley: it turns up everywhere, in every dish, from the antipasto to the dessert. It adapts to thousands of uses: it can be drunk, poured or sprinkled, particularly when the occasion is special.

CROSTINI DI POLENTA CON SALSICCE

Cornmeal slices with sausages

Many qualities of cornmeal are available on the market nowadays, from coarse Bramata to very finely ground Monte Amiata.
I myself do not much care for the coarse type because the mixture turns out heavy and rather too "rough-and-ready" for me. For this "crostino", I would use a medium-ground, bright yellow flour which has not been mixed with other starches.

Make a fairly thick porridge, stirring with a wooden spoon over a low flame for about 40 minutes.
Separately, sauté the onion with the spring onions in a trickle of oil in a pan.
Add the crumbled sausages and raise the heat to cook the mixture through. Add the coarsely-chopped tomatoes and allow to reduce appreciably.
Place the cooked cornmeal on a pastry board (or else in a rectangular oven tray which is much more practical) and leave to cool.
Cut into rectangles which are not too thin and deep fry them in oil.
When they are very crisp and golden, liberally spread the mixture over them and serve hot.

These tasty "crostini" are for serving up especially in the winter, when the frying and consumption of a hot dish do not require too much of an effort.
Not everybody manages to fry polenta without it crumbling.

There is a trick and, like all tricks, it is simple. Everything depends on letting the cornmeal slices colour nicely on each side before turning them and on maintaining a high oil temperature.

300g / 11 oz cornmeal
1 red-skinned onion
2 spring onions
2 tomatoes
3 sausages
olive oil

Servings: 4
Preparation time: 20′+30′
Cooking time: 40′+50′
Difficulty: ●●
Flavour: ●●
Kcal (per serving): 672
Proteins (per serving): 20
Fats (per serving): 39
Nutritional value: ●●●

FETTE COL CAVOLO NERO

Toast with kale

2 bunches of dark green cabbage or kale
stale bread
olive oil
freshly ground pepper
lemon, 2-3 garlic cloves

Servings: 4
Preparation time: 15′
Cooking time: 30′
Difficulty: ●
Flavour: ●●●
Kcal (per serving): 215
Proteins (per serving): 16
Fats (per serving): 10
Nutritional value: ●●●

Simple to prepare, the outcome (as in the following recipe for "fettunta") is generally acknowledged to be superb, not just by virtue of the very tasty ingredients used, but also because of that minimum but indispensable care taken during the preparation which justifies my drawing up a proper recipe.
Boil the cabbage or kale, stripped of its midribs, for about 20 minutes.
Toast some slices of bread (not too thinly cut) and rub a pared garlic clove over the surface. Serve the toast with the vegetable leaves still dripping water.
Liberally dress with olive oil, a little freshly-ground pepper and a sprinkling of lemon and salt. The flavour can be fully appreciated only if the dish is eaten very hot.

Fettunta

Garlic toast

Cut four slices of firm, crusty bread. Toast them over the fire (marvellous cooked over charcoal, but of course a modern gas or electric grill will do fine), rub a clove of pared garlic over both sides. Finally, drench in olive oil (only Tuscan, of the best quality), sprinkle over a pinch of salt and eat while hot (cold "fettunta" is awful).
If you wish to enjoy "fettunta" as a first course, serve it enriched with ripe tomato slices laid on top, with a sprinkling of chopped basil.

4 slices of white, Italian-style bread
garlic cloves
olive oil

Servings: 4
Preparation time: 10′
Cooking time: 10′
Difficulty: ●
Flavour: ●●●
Kcal (per serving): 205
Proteins (per serving): 15
Fats (per serving): 10
Nutritional value: ●●●

As soon as my children were a year old, their wise grandmother always advised giving them bread and olive oil at tea-time, heedless of pre-digested infant formulas and, more likely than not, of the dictates of a dietetics system rather too prone to TV commercials. And, indeed, she is quite right. Of course, good, simple things never go out of fashion (just like grandmothers)... It is a short step from this to the "fettunta" (literally an "oiled slice"), intended as an antipasto. The time for fettunta is November, with the newly-pressed "olio nuovo", but it is also great in summer (served as an appetiser, at tea-time, whenever you like).

FIORI DI ZUCCA FRITTI

Courgette (zucchini) flower fritters

12 fresh courgette (zucchini) flowers
2 eggs
150g / 5 oz / 1 cup plain flour
olive oil

Servings: 4
Preparation time: 20'+30'
Cooking time: 20'
Difficulty: ●●
Flavour: ●●
Kcal (per serving): 440
Proteins (per serving): 10
Fats (per serving): 31
Nutritional value: ●●●

A popular variation in preparing the batter commonly followed in restaurants big and small, consists in using just the white of the egg and not the whole egg. In this way, the batter is frothier and creates a spectacular effect by forming a kind of "cobweb" over the fries (a similar result can be obtained by adding half a glass of ale to the water). I find, however, that the batter which I have indicated in my recipe is particularly suitable for courgette (zucchini) flowers because it covers them with a light film, making them decidedly crisp and, at the same time, delicate in consistency.

The absolute freshness of the miniature marrow flowers is fundamental to get good results. This means that it is a seasonal dish that you can only enjoy in the spring or summer months, whether you have the good fortune of growing your own vegetables or have to turn to the greengrocer.
Carefully remove the pistil and the small, green, external leaves.
Prepare a batter in the following way: lightly beat the egg with a pinch of salt, add the flour and whisk to remove all lumps. Now add water until a homogeneous, fairly liquid mixture is obtained. Set the batter aside to rest for about 30 minutes.
Dip the courgette (zucchini) flowers into the batter, taking care to hold the flowers upside down for a moment to let the surplus drain off. Deep fry in boiling oil, turning them over cautiously with the aid of 2 forks. It is essential to serve them crisp and piping hot.

Fiori ripieni

Stuffed courgette (zucchini) flowers

Wash the flowers thoroughly; they must be very fresh and rather large. The stuffing is prepared by mixing the béchamel sauce into the minced leftovers from boiled or stewed meat or the raw minced (ground) meat. In the latter case, first sauté in a tablespoon of oil over a fierce heat for ten minutes, allowing to cool before adding to the béchamel sauce. Bind the filling with the beaten eggs, season with salt, pepper and a little chopped parsley. Get the frying pan ready, then open up the flowers with your fingers and fill them very carefully with the stuffing (about a tablespoon for each flower). Roll them in the batter and fry immediately.
A tasty alternative to the forcemeat consists in using mozzarella cheese enhanced with the aroma of a boned, mashed anchovy. Cut up the mozzarella, add the anchovy, 2 tablespoons of béchamel sauce and a handful of stale bread which has been left to soak in milk and then squeezed thoroughly. Bind it all with a beaten egg and then fry the flowers in the usual way.

20 large, fresh courgette (zucchini) flowers
200g / 7 oz lean raw minced (ground) meat, otherwise boiled or stewed meat
coating batter (see recipe on the previous page)
2 eggs
parsley
olive oil

Béchamel sauce:

Milk, 3.5dl / 3/4 pt / 1 1/2 cups
Butter, 20g / 3/4 oz / 1 1/2 tbsp
Plain flour, 20g / 3/4 oz / 1 1/2 tbsp

Servings: 4
Preparation time: 25′
Cooking time: 30′+15′
Difficulty: ●●●
Flavour: ●●
Kcal (per serving): 527
Proteins (per serving): 19
Fats (per serving): 37
Nutritional value: ●●●

For the preparation of the béchamel sauce, gradually blend the flour into the melted butter in a small pan. Season with a pinch of salt and add the milk a little at a time, stirring. Allow to thicken over a medium flame for about twenty minutes.

INSALATA DI BACCELLI E PECORINO

Cheese and broad bean salad

2kg / 4$^1/_2$ lb fresh broad (fava) beans, unshelled
Semi-soft pecorino cheese (unmatured)
1 bunch of catmint or basil
olive oil

Servings: 6
Preparation time: 15′
Cooking time: 10′
Difficulty: ●
Flavour: ●●
Kcal (per serving): 614
Proteins (per serving): 39
Fats (per serving): 27
Nutritional value: ●●●

Take a nice basket of broad (fava) beans (refer to the recipe for braised broad beans on page 106 to appreciate what we mean by the term). Choose them preferably small and fresh (you can tell they are fresh if, on snapping open the pod, they "sing", i.e. they make a sharp, cheerful sound). Shell (removing each footstalk), wash and place them in a saucepan with a trickle of olive oil, a bunch of basil (or catmint) and salt. Cover and bring to the boil for a few minutes. Once cooked, they will appear "wrinkled" but must be al dente or crisp to the bite. Drain and leave to cool. In a vegetable dish, prepare parings of semi-soft, unmatured pecorino cheese to mix with the beans. Pour in 2 tablespoons of olive oil and correct the salt. To give a touch of colour, which is never amiss on the dinner table, add a handful of well-chopped radicchio rosso and a bunch of radishes cut into rounds.

LINGUA ALL'ARANCIO

Tongue with orange

Boil the tongue, with some root vegetables, in plenty of water. The cooking time depends on the size. Draw off the heat when cooked through thoroughly (to test this, pierce the back part with a fork; the tongue will not bleed if cooked, but if it does bleed, return to the heat), skin at once (even if your fingers get burnt!) and leave it to cool completely. Then slice very thinly. Prepare the marinade in a separate dish with the finely-shredded orange peel, the juice and the vinegar and lay the tongue slices on a serving dish, smothering them in olive oil and seasoning with salt and pepper. Set aside to allow the tongue to become impregnated with the flavours, turning the slices carefully from time to time.

1 small calf's tongue
125ml / 4 fl oz / 1/2 cup red wine vinegar
zest (pithless) and juice of 2 oranges
olive oil

Servings: 6
Preparation time: 20'+6h
Cooking time: 1h
Difficulty: ●●
Flavour: ●●
Kcal (per serving): 239
Proteins (per serving): 9
Fats (per serving): 18
Nutritional value: ●●●

Although tongue is generally used as a substantial main dish or is traditionally served on a platter with boiled meat, I suggest using this recipe as an antipasto because the orange marinade lends it a fresh, appetising flavour that is more suitable for the light, elegant impact of an entrée.

PAN DI FEGATI

Liver bread

600g / 1 lb 5 oz chicken, calf's and pig's liver
a few bay leaves
half a large loaf of stale bread
5 whole eggs
60ml / 2 fl oz / 1/4 cup brandy
125ml / 4 fl oz / 1/2 cup milk
a generous knob of butter

Servings: 6
Preparation time: 20'+30'
Cooking time: 2h 30'
Difficulty: ●●●
Flavour: ●●
Kcal (per serving): 870
Proteins (per serving): 60
Fats (per serving): 29
Nutritional value: ●●●

Soak the crustless bread in the milk, then squeeze it well. Trim the liver pieces, cut them up and place with the butter, salt and pepper in a casserole over medium heat for about half-an-hour. Souse with the brandy, allow to evaporate and draw off the heat. Crumble the well-squeezed bread and add to the beaten eggs. Put the liver through the mincer and reduce it to a homogeneous paste. Carefully add the other ingredients.

Lay the bay leaves on the bottom of a rectangular, ovenproof dish to line it uniformly. Slowly pour in the mixture and cook in a "bain-marie" in a moderate oven for about 2 hours. Take it out of the oven, loosen the edges from the dish with a spatula and leave it to cool (but not completely). Turn it out onto a serving dish.

This very refined "antipasto", typical of our traditions, is not really likely to crop up on daily family menus or even on restaurant tables, as it is the prerogative of gastronomic establishments of a certain tenor. This dish can even be served cold, surrounded, perhaps, by some roughly-chopped aspic jelly to give it sparkle and appease the eye. It is, in fact, a major dish which creates a fine effect and befits feast days.

An aerial view of Florence, with the cathedral and Giotto's Bell Tower.

PANZANELLA

Bread salad

1 large loaf of white bread, stale
1 large red-skinned onion
2 large salad tomatoes
abundant basil
olive oil

Servings: 4-6	
Preparation time: 5'+15'	
Difficulty: ●	
Flavour: ●●	
Kcal (per serving): 435	
Proteins (per serving): 11	
Fats (per serving): 10	
Nutritional value: ●●●	

Little else is needed beside some stale white bread. Slice thickly and put to soak in a basin of water. Finely slice the onion and 2 tomatoes into a dish and add 2 handfuls of chopped basil. Squeeze the bread dry (therein lies the secret), add to the vegetables, plus olive oil, vinegar, salt and pepper. Stir to combine all the ingredients thoroughly.

It is a very simple dish, but the bread absolutely must be stale and well-squeezed. "Panzanella" is also very good if eaten straight out of the refrigerator, especially in the summer. Of course, there are other versions (some rather complicated) and most of them require the addition of cucumber. It may be that I do not much appreciate this vegetable, or it may be that "panzanella" has always been made in this way in our household. At the most, I can suggest adding aromatic herbs such as catmint or thyme.

The rolling hills of Tuscany have been portrayed in paintings of all ages.

PESCE FINTO

Mock fish

500g / 1 lb 2 oz yellow, mealy potatoes
1 tbsp tuna fish in olive oil
2 tbsp mayonnaise
10 pickled gherkins
1/2 sweet red pepper
1 black olive

Servings: 4	
Preparation time: 30′	
Cooking time: 30′	
Difficulty: ●●	
Flavour: ●●	
Kcal (per serving): 178	
Proteins (per serving): 4	
Fats (per serving): 8	
Nutritional value: ●●	

This recipe does not merely require the basic ingredients, but also a lot of imagination... Boil the potatoes until they crumble easily and mash them with a fork. When they have cooled down, add the tuna fish (previously drained of oil), the mayonnaise (home-made with lots of lemon). Mix everything together. Season with salt and pepper and then... have fun! Take a long, oblong or round platter; it does not matter which as the "fish" will take on the shape you wish to give it.
Take the mixture in your hands - it's like becoming children again - and shape it into a fish. Slice the pickled gherkins horizontally into quite thin rounds. Starting from the fish's tail, lay them one over the other to create the scales of the fish, then, with the red sweet pepper, make a nice smiling mouth and a long, majestic tail. The black olive forms the mischievous eye.

TONDONE ALL'ALLORO

Bay leaf pancakes

Bay leaf pancakes were meant to "pad out" dinner by completing it and, in some cases, even substituting bread.
The recipe is very simple, but, like most Florentine concoctions, its execution requires time, patience, no hurrying (or "furia" as the Florentine expression has it) and the usual splattering of love.
So then! Finely chop the scented bay leaves (discard those which are nice and young, but which have no aroma). In a bowl, whisk up a thick batter with the white flour gently mixed into the water (be careful of lumps: that is why a whisk is the best thing).
Add the chopped bay leaves and allow the mixture to stand for at least half-an-hour before ladling it into a nice and hot, greased baking pan, letting the "tondone" turn golden brown on both sides.
This is good either hot or cold.

100g / 4 oz / $^{2}/_{3}$ cup plain flour
6 bay leaves
125ml / 4 fl oz / $^{1}/_{2}$ cup water
olive oil

Servings: 4
Preparation time: 10'+30'
Cooking time: 20'
Difficulty: ●
Flavour: ●●
Kcal (per serving): 266
Proteins (per serving): 3
Fats (per serving): 20
Nutritional value: ●●●

TONNO CON LA CIPOLLA E I FAGIOLI

Tuna fish with beans and onion

800g / 1 3/4 lb fresh cannellini or small haricot beans (300g /11 oz if dried)
2 medium-sized red-skinned onions
200g / 7 oz tuna fish in olive oil
olive oil
salt and pepper

Servings: 4-6	
Preparation time: 15′	
Cooking time: 40′	
Difficulty: ●	
Flavour: ●●●	
Kcal (per serving): 554	
Proteins (per serving): 25	
Fats (per serving): 19	
Nutritional value: ●●●	

Boil the beans for forty minutes if they are fresh, or for 2 hours if they are dried and have previously been soaked for half an hour. For the correct procedure for cooking beans, please see the relative recipe.
Cut the onion up finely and add to the tuna fish (that you will have flaked) in a bowl. Add the cold, well-drained beans. Season with olive oil, salt and freshly-ground pepper.

Salsa alla toscana

Tuscan sauce

50g / 2 oz/ 4 tbsp lard
1 onion
1 stalk of celery
1 carrot
50g / 2 oz boiled, unsmoked ham
one *boletus edulis* mushroom
1/2 l /1 pt / 2 1/4 cups meat stock
knob of butter
olive oil

Servings: 4
Preparation time: 20'
Cooking time: 30'
Difficulty: ●●
Flavour: ●●
Kcal (per serving): 318
Proteins (per serving): 4
Fats (per serving): 31
Nutritional value: ●●●

Melt the lard in a saucepan and add the finely-chopped onion, celery and carrot.
When all the vegetables are lightly coloured, add the ham cut into strips, with the fat discarded. Stir and season with salt and pepper.
Now add the *boletus edulis* mushroom (carefully wiped clean of all dirt with a damp cloth and sliced paper thin) and the stock. Simmer gently for 15-20 minutes, stirring frequently with a wooden spoon to blend all the ingredients really thoroughly.
Skim off the fat and sieve the sauce. Return to very low heat and, if necessary, add a knob of butter to bind the sauce together.

SALSA DI POMODORO

Tomato sauce

2kg / 4 1/2 lb ripe tomatoes
2 onions
1 carrot
2 celery stalks
olive oil

Servings: 4-6
Preparation time: 10'
Cooking time: 30'
Difficulty: ●●
Flavour: ●●
Kcal (per serving): 163
Proteins (per serving): 3
Fats (per serving): 10
Nutritional value: ●

Wash the tomatoes, cutting out any blemished parts. Chop roughly and place in a large saucepan with the other vegetables, chopped. Heat slowly to boiling point over a moderate flame. Periodically, skim off the excess juices with a ladle (this will depend on the quality and ripeness of the tomatoes), leaving only the red, juicy pulp of the tomatoes to cook along with the other vegetables. When the mixture has broken up, lower the flame and drizzle a thin stream of oil into the pan, adding a pinch of salt. Continue cooking for twenty minutes. Then leave to stand a little and pass the sauce through a vegetable mill. Allow to cool completely and pour into air-tight jars. If in season, a sprig or two of basil could be added during the cooking stage, while a few whole, fresh leaves are placed in each jar to remind you of summer through the encroaching winter, which will be less tedious if brightened up with the aromas and colours of summer entrapped in your little jars.
"Florentine" tomatoes (i.e. those tubby, rather ungainly ones which are a bit like apples in shape, or rather, like miniature pumpkins) are the ones I would use, because they are sweet and rich in juicy pulp. I hold that they are highly suitable for making a sauce, even more so than the canonical Neapolitan plum tomatoes, all smooth and roughly olive-shaped. If you do not live in Florence or round about, you will have to find something suitable in replacement of my adored "fiorentini".

SALSA VERDE

Green parlsey sauce

Rinse the parsley and chop all ingredients finely after draining the capers of their preserving liquid. Place the ingredients in a bowl with 4 tablespoons of olive oil, the vinegar and a pinch of thyme, going easy on the latter because its strong flavour tends to smother the other ingredients. Blend the sauce well by stirring and correcting the quantity of vinegar. Serve with boiled meat or as a tasty spread on rounds of fresh, untoasted bread.

bunch of parsley
100g / 4 oz/ 1/2 cup pickled capers
3 eggs, hard-boiled
a pinch of thyme
1-2 tablespoons of red wine vinegar
olive oil

Servings: 4
Preparation time: 15′
Difficulty: ●
Flavour: ●●●
Kcal (per serving): 209
Proteins (per serving): 8
Fats (per serving): 16
Nutritional value: ●●●

SALSA VERDE ESTIVA

Summer green sauce

Use only the leaves of the herbs, which are to be rinsed under the tap and dried in a clean tea towel. Shell the eggs and combine the ingredients in an electric blender, binding with the butter (softened at room temperature) and a few drops of lemon juice. Season with salt and pepper, taking care not to overpower the delicate aromas of the herbs. This is excellent served with meat, even grilled, or boiled vegetables, particularly potatoes.

bunch each of catmint, parsley, mint and basil
2 eggs, hard-boiled
100g / 4 oz/ 1/2 cup butter
1 lemon

Servings: 4
Preparation time: 15′
Cooking time: 7′ (for the eggs)
Difficulty: ●
Flavour: ●●
Kcal (per serving): 308
Proteins (per serving): 7
Fats (per serving): 30
Nutritional value: ●●●

There are umpteen variations of this sauce. The recipe I have just described is apt for the summer season, when wild mint can easily be found on the roadside in country lanes, or else in a good greengrocers for those who are not so expert.

Sugo con le olive

Olive sauce

100g / 4 oz/ 1/2 cup + 2 tbsp each of sweet black olives, green olives in their seasoning liquid and garlicky green olives
50g / 2 oz/ 5 tbsp garlicky black olives
4 red-skinned onions
2 cloves of garlic
1l / 1 3/4 pt / 4 1/2 cups puréed fresh or tinned (canned) tomato
olive oil
chilli pepper

Servings: 6
Preparation time: 20′
Cooking time: 1h 20′
Difficulty: ●●
Flavour: ●●●
Kcal (per serving): 336
Proteins (per serving): 5
Fats (per serving): 27
Nutritional value: ●●●

Chop the onions roughly and brown in 8 tablespoons of olive oil in a saucepan.
Meanwhile carefully pit both green and black olives, cut into reasonably-sized pieces and add to the onions when these have turned golden. Cook gently over medium heat for about a quarter-hour, stirring with a wooden spoon, so that the olives are fully blended with the onions.
Then add the tomato purée or tinned tomatoes. Continue cooking over medium heat, stirring frequently, and season with salt and lots of chilli pepper. Simmer for about an hour.
This delicious sauce is perfect with short pasta, particularly pennette and rigatoni, which combine with it better, because, as both types are shaped like small tubes, the sauce is trapped inside besides coating the outside.

PASTA, SOUP AND RICE DISHES

2

Acquacotta

3 red-skinned onions
1 yellow sweet pepper
1 stalk of celery
3 ripe tomatoes
stale white bread (8 slices)
3 egg yolks
semi-ripe pecorino, grated
olive oil

Servings: 4
Preparation time: 15′
Cooking time: 1h 15′
Difficulty: ●●
Flavour: ●●●
Kcal (per serving): 560
Proteins (per serving): 20
Fats (per serving): 17
Nutritional value: ●●●

Cut up the onions, pepper and celery. In a frying pan, sauté the onion in oil until golden, then add the pepper, celery and the tomato pulp and leave to cook slowly for about an hour. Transfer everything to a casserole (preferably in earthenware) and add about a litre (1 3/4 pints / 9 cups) of water. Leave to boil about ten minutes more. Meanwhile, set out some soup bowls with slices of toast laid on the bottom, fill with the "acquacotta". Place a yolk in each bowl, taking care not to let it break. Leave to stand for a moment, sprinkle over the grated pecorino cheese, then serve.

A cowboy of the Maremma; in the background, a beautiful sunset on the Nature Reserve Uccellina.

The elderly lady who provides me with freshly-laid eggs seems to have stepped out of an antique print: she is all wrinkles with a large handkerchief on her head. We have a proverb which runs, "A newly-laid egg is worth a ducat". My version of "acquacotta", a dish originating in the Maremma district of Tuscany, is extremely simple as regards the ingredients and the preparation. There are more complex and "spectacular" recipes, but I truly believe that mine has the merit of being delicious, yet not too laborious.

1kg / 2 1/4 lb onions
150g / 5 oz peas and other garden vegetables
1 head of celery
1 carrot
1/2 l / 1 pt / 2 1/4 cups chicken stock
white bread
125ml / 4 fl oz / 1/2 cup white wine
olive oil
Parmesan cheese

Servings: 4
Preparation time: 15′
Cooking time: 55′
Difficulty: ●●
Flavour: ●●
Kcal (per serving): 412
Proteins (per serving): 14
Fats (per serving): 11
Nutritional value: ●●

Carabaccia ▸

Onion soup

Chop the celery, carrot and onion up finely, and cook in a casserole (preferably one in earthenware) with 6 tablespoons of oil.
Sauté gently for about 40 minutes until the vegetables have completely expelled all their liquid.
Then toss the peas into the casserole and finish cooking.
Toast the bread, dunk it in boiling water and, after laying a slice in the bottom of each diner's soup bowl, pour over the "carabaccia", finishing off with a liberal dusting of Parmesan cheese.

400g / 14 oz chicken livers
cock's testes and combs, hen's unlaid eggs
3 egg yolks
50g / 2 oz / 4 tbsp butter
1 onion
white flour
60ml / 2 fl oz / 1/4 cup stock
1 lemon
3-4 sage leaves
ginger

Servings: 4
Preparation time: 30′
Cooking time: 20′+15′
Difficulty: ●●
Flavour: ●
Kcal (per serving): 365
Proteins (per serving): 29
Fats (per serving): 22
Nutritional value: ●●

Cibreo

Chicken giblet casserole

Brown the finely-chopped onion in the butter in a casserole. As soon as it starts to colour, add the giblets. These will consist of the livers well-trimmed of any bile, the cock's testes and the combs previously scalded, skinned and rolled in flour, but not the unlaid eggs which will only be added at the end. Cook over gentle heat, every now and again sprinkling with stock.
When cooked (i.e. after about 20 minutes), take the casserole off the heat, beat the egg yolks with the lemon in a separate bowl and immediately pour onto the giblets. The "cibreo" is technically prepared like a fricassée, but without hesitation I suggest serving it as a first course, considering its incomparable delicacy. It must be served steaming hot and eaten at once.

Over the years, the original recipe of this delicious soup has been modified and simplified (indeed, during the Renaissance period, almonds, sugar, cinnamon and vinegar were added to it).
One could say that this operation of "rationalisation", which goes back centuries and which has been carried out with very many (if not all) dishes belonging to our culinary traditions, has amply succeeded in sharpening the flavour and aroma of the onions and other vegetables in the "carabaccia".
The result is a dish which can confidently compete with any "soupe à l'oignon".
To the "modern" recipe requiring the peas to be pre-cooked (with some left whole and some sieved), I prefer this very personal interpretation of mine, which adds the peas whole as cooking proceeds.
As a final touch, I suggest dunking the bread not just in pure, hot water, but in water to which a glass of white wine has been added, to lend more aroma to this ancient dish and to finish it off nicely.

CRESPELLE ALLA FIORENTINA

Florentine savoury crêpes

the filling:
150g very fresh ricotta of good quality or cottage cheese
2 eggs
200g / 7 oz spinach
a handful of grated Parmesan cheese
pinch of nutmeg

the crêpes:
60g/ 2 1/2 oz / 6 tbsp white, superfine flour
2 eggs
125ml / 4 fl oz / 1/2 cup milk
20g/ 3/4 oz / 1 1/2 tbsp butter

Servings: 4
Preparation time: 20′+30′
Cooking time: 50′+15′
Difficulty: ●●●
Flavour: ●●
Kcal (per serving): 472
Proteins (per serving): 34
Fats (per serving): 34
Nutritional value: ●●●

First of all, cook the spinach, squeeze out all the liquor and put in a bowl together with the ricotta and Parmesan cheeses and a grating of nutmeg. Stir well to combine all the ingredients uniformly into a homogeneous mixture.
Then prepare the batter for the "crespelle", first incorporating the eggs and salt into the flour, then adding the melted butter and the milk. Leave the mixture to stand for at least half-an-hour.
When the crêpes are cooked (in practice they are thin omelettes, fried in a little butter in a small frying pan until set on both sides), spread a little of the cheese and spinach stuffing over each one and roll them up like mini Swiss Rolls.
Grease an oven dish, cover the "crespelle" with béchamel sauce (please see page 17) and dredge with plenty of Parmesan cheese.
If you like, you can even dot with a few splatters of home-made tomato sauce (see relevant recipe). Bake in a hot oven for 20 minutes.

Simple and tasty as they are, these crêpes are, unfortunately, served up nowadays in several ways which are not always correct. At any rate, the original recipe for these so-called "grandmother's kerchiefs" is the one I have described. The only valid variation could be to add aromatic herbs mixed into the spinach to make the crêpes still more delicate. This would only be in summer, however, when the aromas are at their keenest.

GNOCCHI DI PATATE

Potato dumplings

1kg/ $2^1/4$ lb potatoes
250g / 9 oz / $1^2/3$ cups plain flour
2 eggs

Servings: 4
Preparation time: 30′
Cooking time: 40′
Difficulty: ●●●
Flavour: ●●
Kcal (per serving): 493
Proteins (per serving): 17
Fats (per serving): 8
Nutritional value: ●●

Put the potatoes in cold water and bring to the boil. They can be peeled before cooking, if you prefer, to avoid having to handle them when they are boiling hot, but you should be aware that in this way they will not keep their mealy consistency. This is the case, in general.
Boil for half-an-hour over medium heat, drain, peel (protect your hands with a tea towel so as not to get scalded) and mash. Place on a pastry board or on top of the kitchen table.
Blend in the flour a little at a time (not all in one fell swoop), one whole egg, one egg yolk and a little salt.
Work the mixture in your hands until you get a soft pap (be careful that it does not stick to your fingers; if it does, add yet more flour to the mixture, sprinkling it in lightly and progressively mixing it in).
Shape the dough into long sticks that you will cut at an angle into half-an-inch-long strips. As you work, put them on a tea towel and dust with flour.
Boil in lightly-salted water, drain and pour some meat sauce over, or else, quite simply, sage-flavoured butter.
In any case, always dredge liberally with freshly-grated Parmesan cheese before serving at table.

MINESTRA CON LE PATATE

Potato soup

600g / 1 lb 5 oz potatoes
1 red-skinned onion
1 carrot
1 stalk of celery
2 ripe tomatoes
grated Parmesan cheese
white Tuscan bread
60ml / 2 fl oz / 1/4 cup white wine
olive oil

Servings: 4
Preparation time: 10′
Cooking time: 1h 25′
Difficulty: ●●
Flavour: ●●
Kcal (per serving): 444
Proteins (per serving): 13
Fats (per serving): 13
Nutritional value: ●●

In a saucepan, put the potatoes cut into chunks, together with the other vegetables in 6 tablespoons of oil. Bring gently to the boil and then add about a litre and a half (2 1/2 pints / 6 3/4 cups) of water, salt, pepper and the white wine.
Simmer for about an hour, adding 2 tablespoons of oil half-way through.
Pass through the vegetable mill and return to the heat for twenty minutes more.
Toast the bread slices, dice (if you wish, the bread cubes can be fried in olive oil) and put a handful in each person's bowl.
Dust generously with Parmesan cheese.

MINESTRA DI CECI E PEPERONI

Chickpea (garbanzo) and pepper soup

Soak the chickpeas (garbanzos) overnight in cold water with a tablespoon of bicarbonate of soda (baking soda) and one of coarse sea salt.
Rinse thoroughly in cold, running water, then place in luke-warm water in a saucepan and heat. Add strips of bacon, the bay leaves and the thyme. Cover and cook slowly for 2 hours.
Put the finely-chopped onion in a saucepan and sauté in 6 tablespoons of oil. As soon as it turns a golden colour, add the diced potatoes, the peppers (washed, seeded and cut into strips), the finely-chopped carrot and the tomatoes in chunks. Bring to the boil and cook for a quarter-hour over moderate heat, constantly stirring with a wooden spoon.
The moment the chickpeas are cooked, pour the prepared sauce into them, stirring gently.
Serve in soup bowls with a sprinkling of chopped parsley on top.
This fine soup, indeed distinctive on account of the original *concordia discors* of its flavours, is only good when served piping hot.

300g / 11 oz / 2 cups chickpeas (garbanzos)
100g / 3 1/2 oz smoked bacon
1 red-skinned onion
1 red and 2 green sweet peppers
1 carrot
2 potatoes
3 ripe tomatoes
2 bay leaves
a little thyme
1 clove of garlic
parsley
olive oil

Servings: 4-6
Preparation time: 15'+8h
Cooking time: 2h ca
Difficulty: ●●
Flavour: ●●●
Kcal (per serving): 927
Proteins (per serving): 21
Fats (per serving): 63
Nutritional value: ●●●

MINESTRA DI FARRO

Emmer (wheat berry) soup

200g / 7 oz / $1^{1}/_{4}$ cups emmer (wheat berry)
200g / 7oz dried borlotti beans
half an onion
rosemary, sage
2 cloves of garlic
4 slices of Continental bread
olive oil

Servings: 4
Preparation time: 15'+6h
Cooking time: 1h 40'
Difficulty: ●●
Flavour: ●●
Kcal (per serving): 582
Proteins (per serving): 25
Fats (per serving): 12
Nutritional value: ●●

Soak the beans for 5-6 hours. Drain, reserving the soaking water. Place in cold water and, over a very low flame, with the saucepan cover on, bring to the boil for a good half-hour. In the meanwhile, chop the onion, garlic, rosemary and sage finely and let it all colour slightly in 5 or 6 tablespoons of olive oil in a saucepan. Add the emmer and "toast" for a few minutes. Then pour over the water you have kept aside and simmer for a good hour.
Halfway through cooking time, throw in three quarters of the beans. Rub the rest through a sieve or vegetable mill, and add this purée at the end to give the soup bulk.
Allow to rest a few minutes, then serve with a sprinkling of freshly ground pepper. Drizzle over a trickle of unrefined olive oil and dunk a slice of Continental bread (toasted and rubbed with a clove of garlic) in the dish.

There used also to be pine-nuts in the traditional, age-old recipe, to be added along with the Parmesan before baking, probably to give it a summer touch. This recipe is characteristic of St Lawrence's feast day on 10 August, a date which the Florentines particularly cherish, full of Medicean reminiscences, as well as being known as the night of falling stars. It would even seem that this dish was so loved by Lorenzo the Magnificent's fellow citizens that they forgot all about the poor martyr roasted on the grid-iron and instead called that day the "Festa della porrea" (this possibly gave rise to the Italian term "purea" and subsequently to their "purè").

MINESTRA DI PORRI

Leek soup

1kg / 2 1/4 lb leeks
2 tbsp plain flour
1/2 l / 1 pt / 2 1/4 cups stock
continental bread
parmesan
olive oil

Servings: 4
Preparation time: 10'
Cooking time: 1h ca
Difficulty: ●●
Flavour: ●●
Kcal (per serving): 376
Proteins (per serving): 12
Fats (per serving): 13
Nutritional value: ●●

Trim the leeks, slice and cook gently in 6 tablespoons of oil in a pan. Be careful not to fry them, but let them cook slowly, turning them often with a wooden spoon.
When they are cooked, remove from the heat and add the flour, little by little, stirring continuously until the flour has been completely absorbed.
Pour on the stock (not boiling) and leave to cook over medium heat for another half-hour, until the leeks disintegrate.
Toast 6 slices of Tuscan bread, place in a baking dish, cover with the leek mixture and dust generously with grated Parmesan.
Bake in a hot oven for about 10 minutes.

MINESTRONE

Vegetable soup

200g / 7 oz fresh white beans (100g / $^1/_4$ lb if dried)
2 red-skinned onions
2 carrots
2 stalks of celery
2 potatoes
3 courgettes (zucchini)
swiss chard
$^1/_4$ savoy cabbage
200g / 7oz / 1 cup + $1^1/_2$ tbsp rice
stock
olive oil

Servings: 4-6
Preparation time: 15′
Cooking time: 1h 20′
Difficulty: ●●
Flavour: ●●
Kcal (per serving): 300
Proteins (per serving): 9
Fats (per serving): 11
Nutritional value: ●●

Fry the onion, finely-chopped, and the other vegetables, diced, in 8 tablespoons of oil over medium heat, stirring often with a wooden spoon.
Keep the saucepan covered so that the vegetables 'sweat' in their own juice as long as possible. As soon as you see that the juice seeping out is no longer sufficient, add enough water to completely cover them. Leave to cook slowly for about an hour, with the lid on, seasoning with salt and pepper.
Then add the rice and boiling water to submerge everything again. Stirring frequently, simmer gently for another 15 to 20 minutes.

If made with rice, the minestrone is really only good served hot, but if you substitute the same amount of maccheroncini or pennette (both very short kinds of pasta), it is excellent eaten cold (on a summer's evening perhaps), with a nice bunch of fresh, fragrant basil finely chopped over your soup plate.

Minestrone con la salvia

Vegetable soup with sage

250g / 9 oz fresh or dried borlotti beans
100g / 4 oz pappardelle
a handful of dried *boletus edulis* mushrooms
a clove of garlic
a bunch of chopped sage
1 ripe tomato
olive oil

Servings: 4
Preparation time: 15'+15'
Cooking time: 20'+40'
Difficulty: ●●
Flavour: ●●●
Kcal (per serving): 262
Proteins (per serving): 8
Fats (per serving): 10
Nutritional value: ●

In a large saucepan, brown the garlic, sage and mushrooms (previously soaked in luke-warm water) in 3 tablespoons of oil.
Add the tomato, the cooked beans (you will remember to soak them first if they are dried, won't you?), mashed in a vegetable mill, and their cooking water.
Season with salt and pepper and add the pappardelle. Cook gently until the soup is thick and tasty.
This dish should also be served with a trickle of crude olive oil as a final touch.

Other types of pasta could take the place of the pappardelle, i.e. maccheroncini or small ribbed penne (pennette rigate), so long as they are made of durum wheat.
If the soup is cooked in less water, you will obtain a "ragù" to serve over a dish of pasta. This is a slightly more modern interpretation of an ancient peasant dish which was, of course, once eaten as a complete meal, but its "heaviness" may not be appreciated nowadays.

Pappa al pomodoro

Tomato bread soup

For perfect results, assemble all the ingredients first because, though simple, this dish needs both very little cooking and a speedy preparation with no interruption or change of mind and mistakes are not allowed.
In a large saucepan, sauté the garlic gently in 4 tablespoons of olive oil. As soon as it turns golden, toss in the peeled tomatoes and a nice bunch of basil, all roughly chopped, and finally the thickly-sliced bread. Bring to the boil for a moment, adding the water or (if you like a smoother, fuller flavour) the vegetable stock so that you get a dense mush without the bread disintegrating.
Be careful, however, of the amount of juice exuded by the tomatoes; it does not go without saying that you absolutely must add all the liquid, be it water or stock.
Season with salt and pepper. That's all! Lift the lid and you will savour all the aromas of summer; close your eyes and you will see the blue Italian sky and will hear the cicadas drone.

I adore this dish. I am horrified if it is proposed in the winter (where to find the scented basil and the ripe tomatoes which are essential for its successful outcome?). I realise that outside Tuscany you cannot be so fussy. But my advice is to try and get as close as possible to the same quality of ingredients and the same preparation techniques described here. Some people suggest leeks as a substitute for the garlic, others sieve it all before serving with crude olive oil. I hold that the basic recipe that I am presenting is the most balanced. By the way, it is delicious either hot or cold, but never dredged with Parmesan cheese.

250g / 9 oz stale, white, Tuscan-style bread
1l / $1\frac{3}{4}$ pt / $4\frac{1}{2}$ cups water or hot vegetable stock
600g / 1 lb 5 oz ripe tomatoes
4 large cloves of garlic
olive oil
bunch of scented basil

Servings:	4
Preparation time:	15′
Cooking time:	35′
Difficulty:	●●
Flavour:	●●●
Kcal (per serving):	281
Proteins (per serving):	7
Fats (per serving):	10
Nutritional value:	●

PAPPARDELLE SULLA LEPRE

Pappardelle with hare sauce

Prepare the pasta with the flour, the whole eggs and the olive oil (which is missing from the "ordinary" pappardelle recipe). Work it in your fingers and roll it out. Leave for half-an-hour and cut it into long strips an inch wide. To make the sauce, use only the forequarters of the hare. Collect all the animal's blood because you will need it in substitution of the tomatoes (this is how they used to make this and other dishes before 1492).
Joint and add to the pan where the onion is browning in the oil. Over a slow flame, let the juices run out of the meat and add the parsley and other vegetables with the chopped offal. Allow the flavours to blend and then douse with red wine and the blood, and reduce. Remove the hare joints from the pan and bone them. Return the boned meat to the sauce and leave it to cook for a few minutes more. Boil the pappardelle in salted water until cooked but firm to the bite and serve very hot, generously seasoned with the sauce, and sprinkle over some grated Parmesan.

This recipe today can only be attempted by those few who come by a sufficiently-matured, fresh hare (and not frozen or imported as almost always is the case). Whether it is because the hunting of them is limited or even forbidden by law, or whether it is because this species is now scarcely encountered on Tuscan territory, this dish has become a choice delicacy of gourmands of our cuisine.

the hare sauce:

1 small, young hare with heart, liver, lungs, etc.
2 carrots
1 onion
celery
parsley
red wine
1 tbsp olive oil

the pappardelle:

400g / 14 oz / 2^2/3 cups superfine plain flour
3 whole eggs
a tablespoon olive oil

Servings: 4
Preparation time: 30'+30'
Cooking time: 1h 20'
Difficulty: ●●●
Flavour: ●●
Kcal (per serving): 693
Proteins (per serving): 34
Fats (per serving): 20
Nutritional value: ●●●

Typical Tuscan farmhouses in the Siena district.

PAPPARDELLE AL CONIGLIO STRASCICATO

Pappardelle with rabbit sauce

1 rabbit weighing 1.2 kg / 2 lb 10 oz
onion, carrot, celery
3 ripe tomatoes
a little thyme
parsley
350g / 3/4 lb pappardelle (see previous recipe)
olive oil

Servings: 4	
Preparation time: 15′	
Cooking time: 1h ca	
Difficulty: ●●	
Flavour: ●●	
Kcal (per serving): 549	
Proteins (per serving): 34	
Fats (per serving): 16	
Nutritional value: ●●●	

Rinse the rabbit and joint, leaving aside the liver. In a pan, brown the chopped onion, carrot and celery in 6 tablespoons of oil. When it has all coloured, throw in the rabbit joints and sauté over medium heat for 15 minutes. Turn the pieces over frequently with a wooden spoon. Add the peeled tomatoes and the roughly-chopped liver, salt, pepper and savory. Simmer the rabbit in its sauce for half-an-hour over a moderate flame. Draw off the heat and remove to a dish to cool. Bone and chop up the meat with a "mezzaluna", i.e. a double-handled rocking knife. Return to the cooking juices to boil. Pour this delicacy over pappardelle (home-made if possible) which become better impregnated with the sauce. Serve boiling hot, garnishing the tureen with sprigs of fresh parsley which you will also chop finely over the pasta.

350g / 3/4 lb pappardelle (see recipe on page 47)
1/2 duck, with heart and liver
400g / 14 oz tomatoes
onion, carrot and a stick of celery
parsley
white wine
grated Parmesan
olive oil

Servings: 4	
Preparation time: 15′	
Cooking time: 1h 30′	
Difficulty: ●●	
Flavour: ●●	
Kcal (per serving): 647	
Proteins (per serving): 36	
Fats (per serving): 22	
Nutritional value: ●●●	

PAPPARDELLE SULL'ANATRA ▸

Pappardelle with duck sauce

Gently fry the chopped vegetables (with the exception of the tomatoes) in 6 tablespoons of oil, then toss in the jointed duck (plucked, drawn, cleaned out, wiped and singed as usual). Brown, then add the white wine. Cover and leave to cook for 15 minutes. Add the tomatoes (tinned ones are fine), cook a further hour over low heat. Remove the duck from the pan, bone it as soon as possible and return the meat to the sauce with the roughly-chopped liver and heart. Bring to the boil once more and season with salt and pepper. Cook the pappardelle in salted, boiling water until "al dente" (about 10 minutes), serve with the steaming sauce poured over and dust with grated Parmesan. Alternatively, sprinkle a handful of fresh, finely-cut chives over the pappardelle and, in season, garnish each plate with chive flowers.

Siena: a view down Via Sant'Agata; the Torre del Mangia soars up in the background.

PASTA E FAGIOLI

Beans and pasta

Cook the beans over gentle heat for 40 minutes (for an hour-and-a-half if they are dried, after soaking for 2 hours covered in water), with the herbs and garlic to lend flavour and aroma. Then, either sieve or pass through a vegetable mill, so as to eliminate the outer husks. Place the purée in a saucepan, season with salt, pepper and a little chilli pepper to taste. Cook the pasta in the purée and add a little water to finish cooking.

This famous "soup" absolutely must be served hot with a "C" trickled over the surface in olive oil. The original recipe advises cooking the beans in an earthenware pot in a slow oven for several hours (about 3). I find, however, that excellent results are obtained if the ancient recipe is streamlined and adapted to modern rhythms, unfortunately faster and more pressing even in the kitchen.

200g / 7 oz rigatoni (short, fluted noodles)
700g / 1 1/2 lb cannellini beans (300g / 11 oz if dried)
2 cloves of garlic
1 sprig of sage
1 sprig of rosemary
olive oil
chilli pepper

Servings: 4
Preparation time: 15′+2h
Cooking time: 30′+40′
Difficulty: ●●
Flavour: ●●●
Kcal (per serving): 452
Proteins (per serving): 15
Fats (per serving): 10
Nutritional value: ●●

RIGATONI STRASCICATI

Rigatoni sautéed in sauce

First of all, prepare the meat sauce by chopping up all the vegetables (except the tomato) and browning them in 6 tablespoons of olive oil. When they have taken on colour, add the meat, raise the heat and cook over a medium flame for about 15 minutes, stirring frequently with a wooden spoon. Add the tomatoes, season with salt and pepper and leave to simmer very gently for an hour (but it is fine if you allow it to cook for longer), stirring with a wooden spoon from time to time. Cook the rigatoni in plenty of salted, boiling water and drain when the pasta is practically half-cooked. Put the ragù into a large saucepan, pour in the rigatoni and allow to finish cooking - the Italian term "strascicati" means "dragged through the sauce".

350g / 3/4 lb rigatoni
300g / 11 oz lean minced (ground) meat
1 rather large red-skinned onion
1 stick of celery
1 carrot
5 ripe tomatoes or 1/2 l / 1 pt/ 2 1/4 cups home-made tomato sauce
olive oil

Servings: 4
Preparation time: 20′
Cooking time: 1h 30′
Difficulty: ●●
Flavour: ●●
Kcal (per serving): 583
Proteins (per serving): 26
Fats (per serving): 17
Nutritional value: ●●●

300g / 11 oz / 2 cups cornmeal
2-3 bunches of Tuscan 'black' cabbage or kale
olive oil
bacon

Servings: 4
Preparation time: 15'
Cooking time: 30'+40'
Difficulty: ●●
Flavour: ●●●
Kcal (per serving): 469
Proteins (per serving): 7
Fats (per serving): 22
Nutritional value: ●●●

Polenta col cavolo nero

Cornmeal and kale

For about 20 minutes, cook the wrinkled leaves of the 'black' cabbage (actually dark green) - but kale or collard will be fine - which will previously have been rinsed in running water and the midribs stripped off and discarded. Drain, preserving the cooking liquor. Into the latter you will gradually pour the cornmeal flour and let it cook slowly for about 40 minutes, stirring constantly with a wooden spoon so that unpleasant lumps do not form. In another pan, fry the diced bacon. When reduced, add the cabbage. When the polenta is almost ready, add the cabbage and bacon and serve immediately, if you like it hot.
Otherwise, when it has completely cooled down after transferring to an ovenproof dish, cut it up into half-inch slices and put under the grill.

POLENTA PASTICCIATA

Cornmeal pie

In a large pan, sauté all the finely-chopped vegetables with 4 tablespoons of oil. Stir frequently with a wooden spoon for about 10 minutes over low heat, then add the minced (ground) meat, raise the flame a little and brown. After about 20 minutes, add the tomato sauce, salt, pepper and a teaspoon of chilli pepper paste.
Continue cooking very gently and in the meantime prepare the polenta.
Bring two litres (3 1/2 pints / 9 cups) of water to the boil, draw off the heat and, with the aid of a wooden spoon or, even better, of a whisk, shower in the cornmeal flour, stirring continuously so that lumps do not form.
Return to very low heat for about 40 minutes and, meanwhile, prepare the béchamel sauce.
Finish cooking the polenta, turn it out onto a pastry board (make sure that it is no thicker than 1/2 inch) and allow to cool, while the meat sauce is simmering away.
Cut into squares and arrange a layer in a large, buttered ovenproof dish.
Alternate layers of polenta with 5 tablespoons of ragù and a handful of Parmesan cheese.
Continue in this way until the dish is full. Spread a generous ladle of béchamel sauce over the last layer, dredge with Parmesan and bake in a medium oven for half-an-hour, until a nice golden crust forms on top.

the cornmeal:
500g / 1 lb 2 oz / 3 1/2 cups fine-grain cornmeal

the ragù:
1 onion
1 stick of celery
1 carrot
1l / 1 3/4 pt / 4 1/2 cups home-made tomato sauce
300g / 11 oz lean minced (ground) meat
olive oil
chilli pepper

the béchamel sauce:
50g / 2 oz / 4 tbsp butter
2 tbsp plain flour
1/2 l / 1 pt / 2 1/4 cups milk

Servings: 6
Preparation time: 30'
Cooking time: 1h 30'+40'
Difficulty: ●●●
Flavour: ●●●
Kcal (per serving): 917
Proteins (per serving): 33
Fats (per serving): 36
Nutritional value: ●●●

1 fairly large red-skinned onion
2 carrots
1 stick of celery
4 potatoes
10 courgettes (zucchini)
300g / 11 oz dried beans
bunch of swiss chard
1 savoy cabbage
1 bunch of Tuscan 'black' cabbage or kale
1 leek
tomato purée
2-days' stale Tuscan white bread

Servings: 6	
Preparation time: 20'+5-6h+24h	
Cooking time: 1h 30'+40'	
Difficulty: ●●	
Flavour: ●●	
Kcal (per serving): 753	
Proteins (per serving): 34	
Fats (per serving): 5	
Nutritional value: ●●●	

RIBOLLITA

Réchauffé of bread and vegetable soup

Soak the dried beans and cook over a slow flame. In a pan, gently fry the onion, sliced. Add the other vegetables, diced, with the exception of the cabbage, kale and beans which are added at a later point. When the vegetables have sweated out their juice, cover with hot water and then add all the cabbage and kale, shredded. Cover and simmer for an hour over medium heat. Add the cooked beans (some of them whole and some puréed), salt and pepper. Leave to simmer for another 20 minutes, stirring frequently because the beans tend to stick to the bottom of the pan. Add two or three tablespoons of tomato purée.

Slice the stale bread and, in an earthenware casserole, alternate layers of bread with the soup until the bread is well impregnated. Leave to stand for a day. To serve, remove the desired quantity from the casserole and heat it up or "re-boil" it as the name in Italian suggests.

An unusual shot of the Cathedral of Florence.

RISO AGLI ASPARAGI

Asparagus rice

300g / 11 oz / $1^1/2$ cups + 2 tbsp arborio rice
2 bundles of asparagus
50g / 2 oz / 4 tbsp butter
grated Parmesan cheese

Servings: 4	
Preparation time: 15′	
Cooking time: 40′	
Difficulty: ●●	
Flavour: ●●	
Kcal (per serving): 455	
Proteins (per serving): 11	
Fats (per serving): 16	
Nutritional value: ●●	

Blanche the asparagus in a saucepan deep enough to accommodate it upright, fastened together. Be careful not to completely cover with water, but put the lid on the pan and make sure that steam does not escape from it while boiling (about 20 minutes). Drain the asparagus, reserving the water, then cut it up, ensuring that only the tender (not the stringy) part is used. Melt the butter in a pan and sauté, stirring frequently. Boil the rice in salted water, remove while still "al dente" and mix with the asparagus in the pan, adding half a ladleful of the liquor from the asparagus which you can allow to evaporate. Keep on the heat for a few minutes and serve the rice dredged with the cheese.

RISOTTO AI CARCIOFI ▶

Artichoke risotto

300g / 11 oz / $1^1/2$ cups +2 tbsp rice
6 globe artichokes
40g / $1^1/2$ oz / 3 tbsp butter
200g / 7 oz boiled, unsmoked ham
1 onion
1 lemon
Parmesan cheese
raisin wine
parsley

Servings: 4	
Preparation time: 20′	
Cooking time: 40′	
Difficulty: ●●	
Flavour: ●●	
Kcal (per serving): 787	
Proteins (per serving): 28	
Fats (per serving): 41	
Nutritional value: ●●●	

Trim the artichokes, discarding the tough leaves, and cut into thin wedges. Place in a bowl with water and the lemon. Chop up the onion and sauté slowly in the butter with the ham in strips. Add the artichokes, brown for 10 minutes, then add the rice and a glass of the raisin wine. Stirring with a wooden spoon, cook the rice over medium heat. Begin adding the boiling water (about three quarters of a litre / $1^1/2$ pints / $3^1/3$ cups). When the cooking is finalised (20/30 minutes), season with salt and pepper and, at the moment of serving, beat the rice, pouring in a handful of parsley and lots of grated Parmesan cheese.

TORTELLI DI PATATE

Potato tortelli

First of all, the pasta. Heap the flour into a mound on the table and hollow out the centre into which you will break 5 whole eggs. With much care and patience, gradually work the eggs into the flour.
The result will be a slab of dough that you will shape into a ball and that you will leave under a tea towel to rest while you prepare the filling.
Boil the potatoes in their jackets (in this way they absorb less water). Chop up 2 cloves of garlic and a nice sprig of parsley. Add a ripe tomato, peeled and diced, a generous handful of Parmesan and a pinch of nutmeg to lend aroma.
Then mix it all with the peeled, mashed potatoes, adding salt and pepper and, last of all, a whole, lightly-beaten egg.
Roll out the dough and cut into strips 1 1/2 inches wide. Over half of these, spread 5 or 6 tablespoons of stuffing at well-spaced distances.
Cover each strip with another one of pasta and seal by pressing down well on the borders. Cut each strip into tortelli that you will place on a lightly-floured tea towel as you go.
Boil the tortelli in plenty of salted water, draining off the water when cooked but still firm to the bite. Make sure that the pasta is well-cooked in the thickest part. Serve spread with a good meat sauce and sprinkled liberally with Parmesan cheese.
This is also delicious with just butter and sage, provided that there is always lots of Parmesan.

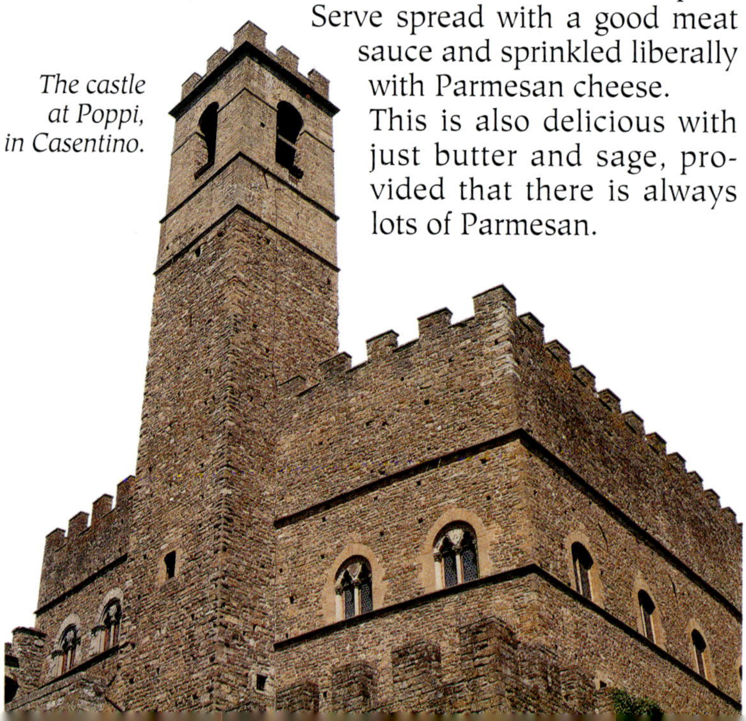

The castle at Poppi, in Casentino.

the pasta:		
the pasta: 500g / 1 lb 2 oz / 3 1/3 cups plain flour 5 eggs *the filling:* 600g / 1 lb 5 oz potatoes	100g / 4 oz / 3/4 cup Parmesan cheese nutmeg garlic parsley 1 ripe tomato 1 egg	**Servings: 4-6** **Preparation time: 40′+30′** **Cooking time: 35′** **Difficulty: ●●●** **Flavour: ●●●** **Kcal (per serving): 810** **Proteins (per serving): 39** **Fats (per serving): 20** **Nutritional value: ●●●**

ZUPPA DI CECI E PANE AGLIATO

Chickpea (garbanzo) soup with garlic bread

300g / 11 oz / 2 cups dried chickpeas (garbanzos)
1 sprig of rosemary
white Italian-style bread
1 rasher of bacon
bicarbonate of soda / baking soda
olive oil

Servings: 4
Preparation time: 20′
Cooking time: 1h 25′
Difficulty: ●●
Flavour: ●●●
Kcal (per serving): 706
Proteins (per serving): 25
Fats (per serving): 25
Nutritional value: ●●●

Soak the chickpeas (garbanzos) - the Mexican type would be better - in 2 litres ($3^1/2$ pints / 9 cups) of cold water in a saucepan, together with a teaspoon of bicarbonate of soda and a handful of coarse sea salt for 8 hours. Cook over a low flame for about an hour and a quarter, adding the bacon rasher half-way through. After that, sieve most of the chickpeas (careful of the husks which must be discarded completely) and keep the remaining whole peas to one side. Toast the slices of bread, rub both sides with garlic cloves and cut into cubes. Separately, heat several rosemary leaves (discard the woody stem) in a tablespoon of olive oil and when they soften up, toss into the soup to which you will have added the whole chickpeas.
Serve the soup with the garlic bread croutons and a trickle of olive oil in each bowl. Do not overdo it as regards the latter because that would make the soup too thick with a "heavy" flavour.

ZUPPA DI FAGIOLI ALLA FIORENTINA

Florentine bean soup

300g / 11 oz fresh cannellini beans (200g / 7 oz if dried)
200g / 7 oz Tuscan 'black' cabbage or kale
4 very ripe tomatoes
1 onion
1 carrot
1 stick of celery
2 cloves of garlic
stale bread
pork rind
1 sprig of rosemary
olive oil

Servings: 4
Preparation time: 15′
Cooking time: 20′+40′
Difficulty: ●●
Flavour: ●●●
Kcal (per serving): 705
Proteins (per serving): 30
Fats (per serving): 18
Nutritional value: ●●●

Cook the beans with the cut-up pork rind in plenty of water. Meanwhile, finely chop the onion, carrot, celery and garlic and brown with the rosemary in lots of oil. Add half a glass of hot water and the tomatoes (or the equivalent amount of tomato paste). When the beans are cooked (40 minutes if they are fresh or 2 hours if they are dried and have been previously soaked), sieve three quarters of them into the saucepan containing the root vegetables and also add the whole ones in their cooking liquid and the pork rind. Boil for another 10 minutes and the soup is ready. Arrange the slices of stale bread (if you like, toast them) in a soup tureen and pour over the soup. Leave to rest a short while and serve warm (but it can also be relished cold).

Here is yet another recipe based on olive oil and bread which allows umpteen variations. For example, there are some who add leeks to the onion, carrot, celery and garlic at the start, but I would prefer perhaps to "summon" the aid of savory, so easy to pick up at the side of a Tuscan country lane.

ZUPPA DI PANE

Bread soup

One ham bone
400g / 14 oz savoy cabbage
3 courgettes (zucchini)
400g / 14 oz bread
200g / 7 oz potatoes
onion, carrot and celery
parsley and basil
600g / 1 lb 5 oz borlotti beans
(300g / 11 oz if dried)
200g / 7 oz tomatoes
olive oil

Servings: 4
Preparation time: 20′
Cooking time: 1h 40′
Difficulty: ●●
Flavour: ●●●
Kcal (per serving): 598
Proteins (per serving): 20
Fats (per serving): 13
Nutritional value: ●●

In a saucepan, sauté the onion with the ham bone (or else with 50g / 2 oz / 4 tbsp of lard) in 6 tablespoons of oil. Cut the other vegetables into pieces, add the parsley and basil, too, and sauté very slowly.
After having cooked the borlotti beans (if fresh, they will need about 40 minutes in plenty of water, whereas dried ones, previously soaked in water, will need about 2 hours over very slow heat), sieve most of them, leaving a couple of tablespoons whole.
Put the bean cooking water in the saucepan with the bone and the vegetables, add the beans (both the purée and the whole ones) and the roughly-shredded savoy cabbage. Cook for about half an hour. Finally, add the very ripe tomatoes (I would prefer "Florentine" tomatoes). Continue cooking for about another quarter-hour and serve the soup nice and hot on slices of stale, toasted bread, finishing off with tracing a "C" in olive oil.

ZUPPA DI PISELLI ALL'OLIO

Pea soup with olive oil

20 white pickling onions
2 teacups stock
1kg / 2 1/4 lb / 4 1/2 cups shelled garden peas
parsley
stale, Italian-style bread
olive oil

Servings: 4
Preparation time: 15′
Cooking time: 50′+10′
Difficulty: ●●
Flavour: ●●
Kcal (per serving): 581
Proteins (per serving): 26
Fats (per serving): 11
Nutritional value: ●●

Sauté the little white onions in 4 tablespoons of oil. Add the stock, stirring with a wooden spoon.
When the onions are a golden colour, add the peas, parsley leaves and more of the stock. Make some bread cubes to fry in 2 tablespoons of oil. Cook the soup over medium heat for three quarters-of-an hour, stirring and seasoning with salt and pepper.
Add the bread croutons last thing, stir rapidly and serve steaming hot, garnishing each soup bowl with fresh parsley sprigs.

Meat and Game

3

ARISTA AL FORNO

Roast loin of pork

1½ kg / 3¼ lb loin of pork on the bone
2-3 cloves of garlic
sprig of rosemary
olive oil
peppercorns

Servings:	6
Preparation time:	15′
Cooking time:	2h ca
Difficulty:	●
Flavour:	●●●
Kcal (per serving):	372
Proteins (per serving):	40
Fats (per serving):	23
Nutritional value:	●●

Take the loin of pork (even if carving becomes more difficult, it absolutely must be on the bone because the taste is indisputably improved) and roll it in chopped rosemary, garlic, salt and pepper. If you like, you can score the meat with a knife and stick some peppercorns in the slits. Grease an oven tin, put in the pork and cook in a slow oven for a couple of hours. While cooking, the meat will exude a tasty gravy that you can cook potatoes in (but also turnips, Swiss chard, cabbage or spinach) to make an excellent, appetising side-dish. This is a dish fit for feast-days and is delicious even eaten cold, carved thinly and washed down with some good red wine.

BRACIOLE DI MAIALE COL CAVOLO NERO

Pork chops with kale

Trim the leaves of the cabbage or kale, stripping them of their midribs, and rinse them. Cook in salted, boiling water for about 20 minutes. Drain well and chop with the aid of a "mezzaluna", i.e. a double-handled rocking knife. With the garlic and finely-chopped onion, brown the chops on both sides in 4 tablespoons of oil in a saucepan, then add the red wine. Cover with the lid and cook over gentle heat for 15 minutes. Remove the meat from the pan and flavour the cabbage or kale in the gravy which has formed. Add the meat and return to the flame for another 10 minutes, stirring continually with a wooden spoon. Season with salt and pepper and serve nice and hot.
Variation: instead of the cabbage or kale, use turnip tops or broccoli, first blanched briefly in boiling water, then broken up and added to the meat.
A typical winter's dish, it likes to be accompanied by a good, sturdy red wine.

4 pork chops, about 150g / 5 oz each
2-3 bunches Tuscan 'black' cabbage or kale
1 red-skinned onion
2 cloves of garlic
125ml / 4 fl oz / 1/2 cup light red wine
whole black pepper
olive oil

Servings: 4
Preparation time: 20'
Cooking time: 50'
Difficulty: ●●
Flavour: ●●●
Kcal (per serving): 392
Proteins (per serving): 32
Fats (per serving): 21
Nutritional value: ●●

BRACIOLE DI VITELLA AI CARCIOFI

Veal chops with artichokes

Trim the artichokes, removing the tougher outside leaves and the internal choke (if there is one). Place in a bowl of water lightly acidulated with a few drops of lemon.
Beat the meat briefly to flatten and allow to stand a while in the egg, beaten with a pinch of salt. Slice the artichokes paper thin.
Stuff each chop by covering about half of the meat with a little cheese and some artichoke slices. Fold over to make a parcel and press down well with your fingers. Dip first in the egg and then in the dried breadcrumbs.
Cook in butter with a pinch of salt and pepper for 15 minutes over medium heat, flipping the parcels over gently to brown them completely on both sides.
Serve the dish really hot, garnished with lemon slices and sprigs of parsley.

4 boned veal loin chops
8 small, tender globe artichokes
1 small lemon
2 eggs
50g / 2 oz / 1/2 cup dry breadcrumbs
100g / 4 oz / 1/2 cup butter
80g / 3 oz fontina cheese

Servings: 4
Preparation time: 30'
Cooking time: 15'
Difficulty: ●●
Flavour: ●●
Kcal (per serving): 724
Proteins (per serving): 40
Fats (per serving): 50
Nutritional value: ●●●

CAPPONE ALLA FIORENTINA

Florentine capon

1 capon - 3kg / 6 3/4 lb
1 medium onion
1 carrot
1 stick of celery
a pinch of savory (fresh if possible)
garlic
2 slivers prosciutto
1 bay leaf
125ml / 4 fl oz / 1/2 cup vinsanto
1/2 l / 1 pt / 2 1/4 cups home-made tomato sauce
1/2 l / 1 pt / 2 1/4 cups stock
stale Tuscan bread
2 knobs of butter
olive oil

Servings: 6
Preparation time: 30′
Cooking time: 2h ca
Difficulty: ●●●
Flavour: ●●
Kcal (per serving): 876
Proteins (per serving): 49
Fats (per serving): 43
Nutritional value: ●●●

Clean and singe the capon, stud it with a few pieces of garlic, savory leaves, a bay leaf and a little salt. Truss the legs and place in 6 tablespoons of oil and a knob of butter in a saucepan, together with the chopped onion, carrot and celery. Brown over fierce heat, frequently basting both with the juices in the pan and the stock that you will have prepared separately (a stock or bouillon cube will do fine).

Continue cooking the capon for half-an-hour, basting every now and then and shaking the pan so that nothing sticks. Add the shredded raw ham and allow to brown before adding the tomato sauce and a pinch of salt and pepper (remember that cured ham is salty) and cook over gentle heat for an hour and a half. Taste the gravy which forms and adjust to taste with the vinsanto. On celebration days, the capon is served up whole on a large dish. Or else it is jointed and arranged on large slices of toast, dipped in the gravy you get from boiling up the cooking juices (when the capon has been removed from the pan) with the addition of half a glass of stock, if necessary.

Nowadays, capons are little exploited at meal times, indeed almost only for the Christmas festivities. It is the great size which makes them suitable for consumption when the company includes large numbers of relatives and friends.

CAPPONE IN AGRODOLCE

Sweet-sour capon

1 small capon
200g / 7 oz / 2 cups walnut kernels
200g / 7 oz / 1 $^1/_2$ cups stoned prunes
100g / 4 oz / $^2/_3$ cups dried figs
100g / 4 oz / $^1/_2$ cup + 2 tbsp stoned green olives
2.5 dl / 9fl oz / 1 cup soured cream
250ml / 9 fl oz / 1 cup vinsanto
1 tablespoon vinegar
150g / 5 oz / $^3/_4$ cup butter
10g / $^1/_4$ oz cloves
salt and pepper

Servings: 4-6
Preparation time: 30′
Cooking time: 1h 35′
Difficulty: ●●●
Flavour: ●●
Kcal (per serving): 1271
Proteins (per serving): 41
Fats (per serving): 99
Nutritional value: ●●●

Clean the capon by drawing, singeing, rinsing under the tap and cutting off the head and claws. Chop all the dried fruit in a bowl, breaking up the walnut halves and the green olives in your fingers, and season with salt, pepper and the cloves.
Mix well by hand, stuff the stomach opening of the capon and sew it up with kitchen string. Melt the butter together with the sour cream and the vinsanto in a large saucepan.
Add the capon, cover the pan and keep over medium heat for an hour and a half. Turn the capon over once only and baste frequently and carefully with its gravy. Should the liquid reduce too much, add a little hot water and a few teaspoons of vinsanto. When the fowl is cooked but very tender, place it on a serving dish and leave to cool for 15 minutes before jointing and serving it with its gravy, which you will have obtained by scraping the bottom of the pan and boiling the cooking juices over fierce heat. Remember to add a tablespoon of vinegar, but only at the last minute.

In Tuscany, this is a triumphant Christmas dish. The original blending of the various flavours jazzes up dinner tables tired of the fowl invariably boiled. The dried fruit and the sour cream flavours marry perfectly.
If the latter is difficult to find, use a rather liquid (not thick) yoghurt.

This was one of Grandfather Luigi's favourite dishes. He, a keen hunter turned into a city dweller, expected his wife to provide it on feast days. This dish originated in the Romagna region of Italy where it was endowed with the aroma of nutmeg, grated over at the last minute and blended in with care.

1 rabbit, about 1 1/2 kg / 3 1/4 lb
onion, carrot and celery
white wine
4 ripe tomatoes
garlicky black olives
white flour

Servings: 4
Preparation time: 20′
Cooking time: 50′
Difficulty: ●●
Flavour: ●●●
Kcal (per serving): 345
Proteins (per serving): 26
Fats (per serving): 18
Nutritional value: ●

Coniglio alla cacciatora

Rabbit cacciatora

Clean the rabbit, joint and coat with flour. Sauté the chopped onion, carrot and celery in a saucepan with 4 tablespoons of oil. When it all begins to colour, throw in the rabbit, except for the liver which will be used elsewhere. Douse with the wine and cook for about 10 minutes over medium heat, stirring with a wooden spoon. Add the chopped tomatoes and some olives, seasoning with salt and pepper. Cook for another 40 minutes over moderate heat.

CONIGLIO ALLA CONTADINA

Rustic rabbit dish

Joint and rinse the rabbit. In a saucepan, brown the chopped onion and cloves of garlic in 4 tablespoons of oil. Add the rabbit joints, drained and dried, together with the liver cut into pieces. Raise the flame and pour a little white wine over, lowering the heat when the liquid has evaporated. Cover with the lid and leave to cook over medium heat for about a quarter-hour. At this point, add the peeled, chopped tomatoes, the rosemary and also 5-6 basil leaves (if you like the fragrance and the season is right). Add salt and pepper to taste. Cook for another 20 minutes, if necessary gradually adding the vegetable stock to maintain the mixture smooth.

1 rabbit, $1^1/_2$ kg / $3^1/_4$ lb
1 red-skinned onion
500g / 1 lb 2 oz ripe tomatoes
rosemary
2 cloves of garlic
white wine
vegetable stock
olive oil

Servings: 4
Preparation time: 20′
Cooking time: 50′
Difficulty: ●●
Flavour: ●●●
Kcal (per serving): 417
Proteins (per serving): 46
Fats (per serving): 22
Nutritional value: ●●

FAGIANO ALLA FIORENTINA

Pheasant, Tuscan style

A pheasant, about 1.3kg / 2 3/4 lb
150g / 5 oz bacon
sage
olive oil

Servings:	**4**
Preparation time:	**20'**
Cooking time:	**45'**
Difficulty:	**●●**
Flavour:	**●●**
Kcal (per serving):	**558**
Proteins (per serving):	**48**
Fats (per serving):	**40**
Nutritional value:	**●●**

Bard the pheasant with thin strips of bacon, after seasoning it inside well with salt and pepper. Truss with kitchen string, put in a baking tin or pan with 4 tablespoons of oil and roast in a hot oven for at least 40 minutes. Baste frequently with the juices in the pan so that the meat does not dry out. When cooked, loosen the string and remove the bacon barding (chopped up, it goes into the juices in the pan to make the gravy). Divide the bird into portions and serve it hot, covered in gravy.

Pheasants that you find in the shops are often already ripened and drawn (i.e. with internal organs discarded). If this is not the case, remove the innards and leave the fowl to mature for a week. (A little time is needed to bring the flavour out.) Pluck it with care (this is a lengthy operation which requires infinite patience!) Cut off the claws and head, singe and rinse the bird in water and vinegar. Now it is ready to be cooked. Thanks to its "trappings", this recipe enables us to appreciate the pheasant cock, even though the flesh is notoriously tougher than his mate's.

FEGATELLI DI MAIALE

Tuscan pig's liver

600g / 1 lb 5 oz pig's liver
200g / 7 oz pork net (caul fat)
bay leaves
laurel twigs for use as skewers
sliced bread
olive oil

Wash the pork net in luke-warm water. Cut the liver into 2-inch pieces and coat with the well-chopped bay leaves, salt and pepper. Cut the net into squares big enough to wrap round the liver pieces. Impale them on the laurel twigs (cut in roughly 8-inch lengths), alternating a liver parcel with a slice of bread (preferably cut from the crusty part of the loaf) and separating them with a bay leaf. Arrange the skewers in a meat tin or baking tray with 5 table-spoons of oil and an additional pinch of salt. Cook in a medium oven for 20 minutes.

Servings: 4
Preparation time: 30′
Cooking time: 20′
Difficulty: ●
Flavour: ●●●
Kcal (per serving): 1035
Proteins (per serving): 40
Fats (per serving): 67
Nutritional value: ●●●

Take care in the cooking; if the liver parcels are left in the oven for too long, they will become tough.
I suggest using laurel twigs because they impart flavour to the meat from the inside.
Lastly, the bread.... You may use any kind of bread you like, but Tuscan-style bread is doubtless the most suitable. You see, our bread is nice and close-textured and, above all, it is not salted, so it will "back up" flavours without altering them. Indeed, it will bring the aroma out.

La Bistecca

T-Bone beef steak

800g / 1 3/4 lb piece of sirloin steak
salt and freshly-ground pepper

Servings: 4	
Preparation time: 5′	
Cooking time: 10′	
Difficulty: ●	
Flavour: ●●	
Kcal (per serving): 400	
Proteins (per serving): 48	
Fats (per serving): 23	
Nutritional value: ●●	

Take the beef steak out of the refrigerator two hours beforehand, otherwise it will suffer in the cooking. Use a barbecue grill, with the charcoal glowing hot, but with no flame. Place the steak on the grill and keep over the fire for 5 minutes until a nice crust is formed. Turn it over (without piercing the meat) and repeat on the other side. The steak will remain over the fire for the time needed just to sear the surface well but keep it nice and rare inside. Season with salt and pepper (better to use freshly ground pepper) and serve at once.
Relish it accompanied by a nice green salad or cannellini beans dressed in oil.

Grazing cattle of Chianina breed.

Originally known as "carbonata" or "cooked over charcoal", the name bistecca comes from the English "beefsteak". This name, apart from the fact that it has become accepted as such, also has an aura of internationality, making it preferable. The success of Florentine beefsteak hangs for the most part on the quality of the meat, but without doubt on the cooking, too. I suggest using oxen of the Tuscan Val di Chiana breed, even though not easy to find. If the cut is right, the result is very good with other cattle stock (provided they have been reared properly). The bistecca must be an inch thick and complete with its T-bone, tenderloin and fillet. This precision is called for beyond the reaches of Tuscany (where it is simply called "fiorentina") as non-Tuscan butchers tend to proffer entrecôtes or rump steak instead of bistecca, the equivalent of visiting a neighbourhood primitive art exhibition instead of the Uffizi Gallery!

FRICASSEA RUSTICA

Veal in a lemon sauce

800g / 1 3/4 lb stewing steak
parsley
2 cloves of garlic
dry white wine
2 egg yolks
1 lemon
100g / 4 oz / 1/2 cup butter
olive oil

Servings: 6
Preparation time: 20'
Cooking time: 1h 30'
Difficulty: ●●
Flavour: ●●
Kcal (per serving): 720
Proteins (per serving): 45
Fats (per serving): 59
Nutritional value: ●●●

Cut up the steak and place in a frying pan with 3 tablespoons of oil, the butter, the parsley (tied in a bunch for easy removal) and the garlic. Cook over medium heat for 20 minutes, basting now and then with the wine. Remove the parsley and garlic and continue cooking an hour longer. Moisten with hot water, if necessary. Then draw the pan off the heat and remove the meat while it is still tender, but not rarely done. Beat the yolks with the juice of a lemon and pour it all into the gravy in the pan. Stir and, if necessary, sprinkle in a little hot water to bind, without returning the pan to the heat. Cover the meat with the sauce and serve.

Half-way through cooking, some cooks add a few dried mushrooms, revived in hot water and then chopped. I approve, provided, of course, that the mushrooms are strictly Boletus edulis.

INSALATA DI TRIPPA

Tripe salad

500g / 1 lb 2 oz tripe
1 white-skinned onion
a fistful of black olives
a fistful of spicy green olives
1/2 red sweet pepper
sprig of parsley
2 lemons
olive oil

Servings: 4
Preparation time: 15'
Difficulty: ●
Flavour: ●●●
Kcal (per serving): 302
Proteins (per serving): 21
Fats (per serving): 22
Nutritional value: ●

Clean the tripe thoroughly and cut into strips half-an-inch thick (or thinner, if you prefer).
Put in a bowl and add the stoned, roughly-chopped olives, the sweet pepper, finely shredded, the onion, cut into rings, and the parsley, chopped. Season with salt, pepper, oil and lemon juice.

*This delectable salad is particularly appreciated in the summer because it is to be consumed cold.
Of course, everyone may add ingredients as they wish to give it a personal touch (e.g. fresh tomatoes in wedges), to round off the flavour (globe artichokes in oil) or to intensify it (e.g. basil leaves instead of the chopped parsley, either roughly torn up in your fingers or left whole as a colourful garnish).*

LESSO RIFATTO

Réchauffé of boiled meat

500g / 1lb 2 oz boiled beef
2 white-skinned onions
300g / 11 oz tinned (canned) tomatoes
a few basil leaves
sprig of sage
olive oil

Servings:	4
Preparation time:	10′
Cooking time:	25′
Difficulty:	●
Flavour:	●●●
Kcal (per serving):	275
Proteins (per serving):	19
Fats (per serving):	19
Nutritional value:	●

Cook the finely-chopped onion gently in 4 tablespoons of oil in a saucepan. Do not let it colour, but allow it to retain its whiteness, covering with the lid and omitting salt.
Once the onions have withered somewhat, add the drained, chopped tomatoes, a little chopped basil and 3 whole sage leaves. Cook for 10 minutes over moderate heat. Now add the sliced boiled meat and bring to the boil briefly to thicken the sauce. Season with salt and pepper. Serve the slices doused in the tasty tomato and onion sauce.

The towered skyline of San Gimignano.

Peposo

Peppered stew

- 500g / 14 oz beef stewing steak
- 6 cloves of garlic
- 3 ripe tomatoes
- 4 slices of stale tuscan bread, toasted
- salt and pepper

Servings:	4
Preparation time:	10′
Cooking time:	2-3h
Difficulty:	●●
Flavour:	●●●
Kcal (per serving):	345
Proteins (per serving):	25
Fats (per serving):	10
Nutritional value:	●

Place the cubed stewing steak in a deep saucepan with the chopped garlic and the tomatoes, skinned and roughly chopped. Season with salt judiciously and with as much pepper as you like (or peppercorns if you prefer). When I say "as you like", I mean a lot of pepper (the dish is not called "peposo" for nothing!), at least a full tablespoon. Pour in enough cold water to cover completely and cook very slowly, stirring from time to time. The dish will only be ready after some hours' cooking, two at least, maybe even three. Serve it all boiling hot over slices of toast. If the stew tends to dry out while cooking, add hot water so that the meat always has a little liquid to cook in.

Market day at Impruneta.

Haste in the kitchen is not in general an ingredient in the production of successful dishes, but, especially in this recipe, I should say that patience is indeed an essential element. In fact, "peposo" stew is indissolubly tied to the vigil watch of the furnace lads at Impruneta, in the hills behind Florence, who used to spend the whole night keeping an eye on the wood-fired ovens where the famous earthenware pots, bricks and vases were cooking. The cooking of "peposo" stew was then even lengthier than it is today, extending over six or even eight hours. The pots of stew were placed at the mouth of the furnace where the red terracotta was hardening and where the heat was low and even.

POLLO ALLA DIAVOLA

Devilled chicken

1 chicken, 1,200g / 2 lb 10 oz
bunch of sage
1 lemon
olive oil

Servings: 4
Preparation time: 15′
Cooking time: 30′
Difficulty: ●
Flavour: ●●
Kcal (per serving): 440
Proteins (per serving): 38
Fats (per serving): 32
Nutritional value: ●●

Clean the chicken by removing the head, claws and insides. Wash and singe it. Open it out like a book, cutting it along the breast bone, and flatten it evenly all over, dusting with salt, pepper and plenty of chopped sage. Grill (broil) over glowing charcoal for a quarter-hour on each side, basting with a brush dipped in olive oil and lemon. Serve hot, accompanied by lots of potato chips.

POLLO AL MATTONE ▸

Chicken underneath a brick

1 chicken, about 1,200g/ 2 lb 10 oz
sage and rosemary
2 lemons
2 cloves of garlic
olive oil

Servings: 4
Preparation time: 15′
Cooking time: 30′
Difficulty: ●
Flavour: ●●●
Kcal (per serving): 440
Proteins (per serving): 38
Fats (per serving): 32
Nutritional value: ●●

Clean the chicken by drawing it, cut off the claws and head, wash and singe it. Open it out like a book, cutting along the breast bone and beating it out, just like in the previous recipe. Chop the herbs finely (if you like, 2 crushed cloves of garlic can be added) and sprinkle over the chicken, brushing with oil. Place on the grill (broiler) over glowing charcoal. While cooking is proceeding over a nice, crackling fire, crush the chicken underneath a heavy clay brick. It should remain so for half-an-hour, during which time you will turn it frequently (without forgetting to baste it with oil and to season with salt and pepper) so that it cooks on both sides, every time covering it up again with the brick. Serve hot and sprinkle liberally with lemon juice.

POLLO FRITTO

Fried chicken

1 spring chicken, about 1,200g / 2 lb 10 oz
3 eggs
150g / 5 oz / 1cup plain flour
olive oil

Servings: 4
Preparation time: 15′+20′
Cooking time: 20′ ca
Difficulty: ●●
Flavour: ●●
Kcal (per serving): 753
Proteins (per serving): 44
Fats (per serving): 28
Nutritional value: ●●●

Cut the chicken into small pieces, rinse and dry. Beat the eggs in a bowl with a pinch of salt, and dunk the chicken pieces in it, leaving them to stand for about 20 minutes. Stir well from time to time so that the chicken is well-impregnated. When you are ready to fry, sprinkle the flour into the bowl and let the egg absorb it thoroughly. It is fundamental that each piece of chicken be well imbued with the mixture. Heat the oil (lots of it and strictly of olives) to the correct temperature in a large frying pan and fry the chicken in it for 20 minutes. Keep the flame low to start with, raising it towards the end to give that final golden colour which is indispensable when frying. Serve with lemon wedges as soon as you have drained off the oil.

POLLO ALLA CACCIATORA ▸

Chicken cacciatora

1 chicken, about 1,200g /2 lb 10 oz
1 onion
1 carrot
1 stick of celery
4 ripe tomatoes
a handful of garlicky black olives
white flour
olive oil

Servings: 4
Preparation time: 15′
Cooking time: 50′
Difficulty: ●●
Flavour: ●●●
Kcal (per serving): 598
Proteins (per serving): 45
Fats (per serving): 39
Nutritional value: ●●

Singe the chicken, wash and draw it. Joint it (there will be about a dozen pieces if the chicken is nice and meaty) and coat with flour. Chop up the onion, carrot and celery and sauté in a saucepan with 4 tablespoons of oil, adding the chicken when the vegetables are on the point of turning golden. Brown for a few minutes over a high flame, turning the joints to impregnate the chicken with the vegetable flavours. Lower the heat and add the chopped tomatoes and olives. Correct for salt and pepper and leave to cook for 40 minutes, turning over the joints from time to time.

Not infrequently is the preparation of this dish enriched with dried mushrooms (previously moistened in water).
I find, however, that the traditional recipe is the winning one as it does not mask the delicate flavour of the chicken meat.
With regard to the name, the origin of which is lost in the mists of time (can you really see hunters or "cacciatori" preparing such a delicacy with grace and patience?), any curiosity will have to remain unsatisfied (at least in this book). However, this is a dish that still today appears fairly frequently on Florentine and Tuscan tables, as it requires little fuss and the preparation time is short.

Sausages and beans,
a strapping, tasty combination,
softened by the aroma
of the sage, garlic and tomato,
ideal for warming up on a cold
winter's evening.
But they are also very good eaten
in the summer,
served up in a buffet,
for example, as the star attraction
among the cold meats, cheeses
and quality wines...

SALSICCE E FAGIOLI

Sausages and beans

Cook the beans for 40 minutes (2 hours if dried, after a 2-hour soaking). Cut the sausages into short lengths and cook in a pan with 2 cloves of garlic and the sage. Cook slowly, piercing them so that they cook right through. They should be cooked, but crisp, not boiled. At this point, add the tomato purée, season with salt and pepper and reduce over moderate heat for a further 10 minutes. Add the beans, draining them well and combine the flavours over gentle heat, stirring carefully with a wooden spoon.

Casks of Brunello di Montalcino wine in a cellar.

400g / 14 oz cannellini beans
5 garlicky, well-seasoned sausages
sprig of sage
1/2 l / 1 pt / 2 1/4 cups puréed tomato
3 cloves of garlic
olive oil

Servings: 4
Preparation time: 15′
Cooking time: 30′+40′
Difficulty: ●●
Flavour: ●●●
Kcal (per serving): 1082
Proteins (per serving): 54
Fats (per serving): 73
Nutritional value: ●●●

SALSICCE E UVA

Sausages and grapes

6 lean, garlicky sausages
bunch of black cooking grapes
50g / 2 oz / 1/4 cup butter
125ml / 4 fl oz / 1/2 cup red wine

Melt the butter in a saucepan. Cut the sausages to pieces (if you can get small, tasty, wild boar sausages, use about ten of them, moistened with a little water to help the cooking along) and brown over a moderate flame for 10 minutes. Swill with wine, add the grapes, bring briefly to the boil and serve nice and hot.

At grape harvesting time, the aroma of sausages cooked with grapes and wine would waft over the air, almost symbolically linking the ongoing harvest to the previous year's. There would be huge, steaming pots on the wooden boards under the portico where everybody tucked in, dunking their bread in the sauce....

Servings: 4
Preparation time: 10′
Cooking time: 15′
Difficulty: ●●
Flavour: ●●
Kcal (per serving): 986
Proteins (per serving): 35
Fats (per serving): 88
Nutritional value: ●●●

SPIEDINI ALLA FIORENTINA

Florentine spit roast

300g / 11 oz pig's liver
200g / 7 oz loin of pork
100g / 4 oz pork net (caul fat)
3 garlicky sausages
stale bread
sage and bay leaves
olive oil

Servings: 4
Preparation time: 30'
Cooking time: 30'+10
Difficulty: ●
Flavour: ●●●
Kcal (per serving): 881
Proteins (per serving): 44
Fats (per serving): 71
Nutritional value: ●●●

Divide the liver into 2-inch cubes. Rinse and soften the pork net in tepid water and cut into small squares for wrapping around the liver pieces. Cube the loin and sausages, as well. Cut the stale bread into fingers, preferably using the crusty side, which will toast nicely when cooked on the spit.
Thread the skewers, systematically alternating the ingredients, and always placing one leaf of bay and one of sage next to the meat cubes (in other words, a slice of bread, bay leaf, liver, sage, bread, bay leaf, loin of pork, sage and so on up the skewer). Season with salt and pepper.
Put the prepared skewers to turn on the spit in front of a fire, brushing frequently with oil. If you do not have a fireplace, use a slow oven, arranging the skewers in a roasting tin with a trickle of oil and only seasoning with salt and pepper when half cooked, at the moment that you turn them.

*These skewers were originally completed with lark, thrush, starling and chaffinch, almost impossible to find nowadays.
Well, not impossible if you are quite happy with just watching them fluttering or hopping around; what is difficult, to the chagrin of hunters and gourmands, is to track them down in a state of decease, ready for the pot.
I remember the fuss that was made in honour of my grandfather's companions in the shooting party when they returned from hunting, with the spit roasts browning in front of the fire while the fat dripped sizzling into the glowing charcoal.*

STUFATO DI VITELLA CON I FUNGHI

Veal stew with mushrooms

500g / 1 lb 2 oz veal stewing steak
1 small onion
2 cloves of garlic
sprig of catmint
300g / 11 oz fresh porcini/ cep mushrooms
1/2 l / 1 pt / 2 1/4 cups puréed tomato
125ml / 4 fl oz / 1/2 cup vegetable stock
olive oil

Servings: 4
Preparation time: 25′
Cooking time: 45′
Difficulty: ●●
Flavour: ●●●
Kcal (per serving): 368
Proteins (per serving): 28
Fats (per serving): 23
Nutritional value: ●

Chop up the onion and garlic and place in a saucepan on the heat with 4 tablespoons of oil. Cube the stewing steak, each piece being the size of a walnut. When the onion begins to colour, add the veal and brown well over fierce heat for 5 minutes, stirring frequently with a wooden spoon. Add the stock and continue to cook over very low heat for a further 20 minutes. Meanwhile, clean the mushrooms thoroughly and slice them paper thin (include the stems, too, if they are unblemished). Now add the tomato purée and the mushrooms to the meat and aromatise with a sprig of catmint. Cook with the lid on for 20 minutes over medium heat, then serve the stew steaming hot. To test whether cooked well enough, prod the meat with a fork. It should feel very tender, otherwise boil the stew up a little more, if necessary adding a few tablespoons of stock. The stew is delicious if served with cornmeal which is rather mushy.

TRIPPA ALLA FIORENTINA ▶

Florentine tripe

1kg / 2$^1/_4$ lb tripe
2 red-skinned onions
2 carrots
head of celery
500g / 1 lb 2 oz tinned (canned) tomatoes
Parmesan cheese
olive oil

Servings: 6
Preparation time: 20′
Cooking time: 1h 20′
Difficulty: ●●
Flavour: ●●●
Kcal (per serving): 465
Proteins (per serving): 47
Fats (per serving): 26
Nutritional value: ●●

Wash the tripe and cut into finger-length strips. Make a mirepoix with 6 tablespoons of oil in a saucepan. Add the tripe and, stirring frequently with a wooden spoon, blend the flavours well. When, after 20 minutes' cooking, some of the liquor has seeped out of the tripe, add the drained tomatoes, salt and pepper and cook for another hour over moderate heat, stirring frequently. Serve the tripe hot, with the addition of Parmesan cheese.

A more luxurious version of this dish encompasses the addition of minced (ground) meat to the mirepoix which is a quarter-cooked before throwing in the tripe. I find that this variation makes the dish a little heavy (it is tasty enough on its own) and that the flavour of the minced meat does not marry well with tripe. However, this dish of ours, known the world over, is still today cooked in Florentine homes, seeing as the raw material, economical and of first-rate quality, is readily available.

TRIPPA BOLLITA NEL VIN BIANCO

Tripe cooked in white wine

1 kg / 2$^1/_4$ lb tripe
4 carrots
2 white-skinned onions
250g / 9 oz / 1$^1/_4$ cups butter
1l / 1$^3/_4$ pt / 4$^1/_2$ cups dry white wine
chopped parsley

Servings: 6
Preparation time: 15′
Cooking time: 2h
Difficulty: ●●
Flavour: ●●
Kcal (per serving): 970
Proteins (per serving): 33
Fats (per serving): 72
Nutritional value: ●●●

Chop the onions and carrots finely into a roomy saucepan and sauté gently in the butter.
When golden, add the tripe, previously washed and shredded.
Cook for 2 hours over low heat, stirring frequently and gradually adding the white wine.
Season with salt and pepper and serve the tripe hot, with a dusting of Parmesan cheese.

VALIGETTE ALLA VERZA

Stuffed cabbage leaves

1 savoy cabbage
400g / 14 oz lean minced (ground) beef or boiled left-overs
1 clove of garlic
2 eggs
1 tablespoon Parmesan cheese
sprig of parsley
300g / 11 oz / $1^1/_2$ cups puréed tomatoes
olive oil
chilli pepper

Servings: 6
Preparation time: 25'
Cooking time: 1h
Difficulty: ●●●
Flavour: ●●
Kcal (per serving): 404
Proteins (per serving): 33
Fats (per serving): 27
Nutritional value: ●●

Discard the external leaves (too woody) of a nice savoy cabbage. Choose some lovely, big leaves with reasonably tender midribs, pull them off the main stem and cook in boiling salted water for 10 minutes. Drain one by one with the aid of a skimmer and lay them out to dry on a tea towel. Make the stuffing with the minced (ground) meat or finely-cut boiled meat, the eggs, the garlic and the chopped parsley. Combine the ingredients and heat over the flame for 10 minutes. Take a spoonful of the mixture and place on each cabbage leaf, which you will then wrap up tightly in your fingers to make firmly-closed parcels.
Arrange them in a saucepan with 8 tablespoons of oil and cook slowly for 20 minutes. Then add the well-drained tomatoes and, turning the "suitcases" over carefully, season with salt and pepper (or chilli pepper) to taste.
Cook for a further 20 minutes. These are very good eaten either hot or cold, perhaps sprinkled with some Parmesan cheese.

I can just picture my mother-in-law's hands in the act of preparing these "suitcases" and pressing them a little to get the stuffing to stick to the leaves. On reading the recipe, some may wonder that I do not suggest binding the parcels with kitchen string, to be removed once cooked. Well, if you are careful, the well-wrapped parcels will stay hermetically closed!

FISH AND SHELLFISH

4

Baccalà alla livornese

Salt cod, Livorno style

800g / 1 3/4 lb salt cod, previously soaked
2 leeks
300g / 11 oz tomatoes
4 cloves of garlic
parsley
white flour
olive oil

Servings: 4
Preparation time: 20′
Cooking time: 20′+20′
Difficulty: ●●
Flavour: ●●●
Kcal (per serving): 300
Proteins (per serving): 37
Fats (per serving): 11
Nutritional value: ●

The most classic of Tuscan recipes for this fish lays down that a tomato sauce (remember to purée the tomatoes) is made with garlic and chopped leeks fried in 4 tablespoons of oil in a saucepan. When the leeks take on a golden colour, add the tomatoes and cook slowly for about a quarter-hour. Cut the fish into at least 6 chunks, bone, coat with flour and deep fry in oil. Allow to colour on both sides over medium heat. Pat dry on brown or kitchen paper, then add to the sauce for a last, brief stewing.
Sprinkle liberally with finely-chopped parsley.
A tasty, rather unusual alternative is to use the "baccalà" as a sauce for spaghetti or thin noodles. In this case, increase the amount of tomato sauce (from 300g to 500g or 600g / 11 oz to 18 oz or 21 oz) and, once the fish has been fried, flake it in your fingers (careful of any bones which may still be around!) and place in the sauce, with a good sprinkling of chilli pepper and parsley. The result will be a rather unusual dish of delicious spaghetti, fragrant and appetising.

Baccalà con i porri

Salt cod with leeks

Bone the fish. Divide into 4 chunks (or even 6), coat in flour and fry in very hot oil until golden on both sides. Drain the pieces on kitchen or brown paper. Rinse the leeks, cut into thin rings. Gently fry them for 10 minutes in four tablespoons of oil in a pan. Add the tomato sauce. The addition of one or two tablespoons of hot water may be necessary to finish off cooking. Add the fish, season with salt and pepper and simmer for a quarter-hour.

800g / $1^3/4$ lb salt cod, previously soaked
4 medium leeks
white flour
300g / 11 oz / $1^1/2$ cups home-made tomato sauce
olive oil

Servings: 4
Preparation time: 20′
Cooking time: 40′+20′
Difficulty: ●●
Flavour: ●●●
Kcal (per serving): 335
Proteins (per serving): 38
Fats (per serving): 11
Nutritional value: ●

This delicious dish is excellent served with polenta.
With reference to the ingredients, I wish to comment on the tomato sauce: most ancient recipes recommend it, whereas nowadays the tomato tends to be excluded so as not to weigh down a dish which is rich on its own.

The Arno and the Ponte Vecchio, in Florence.

BACCALÀ FRITTO

Fried salt cod

800g / $1^3/_4$ lb salt cod, previously soaked
125 ml/ 4 fl oz / $^1/_2$ cup white wine
200g / 7 oz / $1^1/_3$ cups plain flour
chopped parsley
olive oil

Servings: 4
Preparation time: 20′
Cooking time: 5′
Difficulty: ●●
Flavour: ●●
Kcal (per serving): 456
Proteins (per serving): 8
Fats (per serving): 26
Nutritional value: ●●●

Cut the baccalà fillets into pieces and place them in a pan of cold water.
Put on the hob, taking the pan off as soon as it looks like boiling. Drain and pat the fish dry.
The batter is made in the following way: in a bowl, dissolve the flour in the white wine and enough water to obtain a soft, homogeneous mixture. Season with salt and chopped parsley.
Carefully dip each piece of cod into the batter and deep fry in really hot oil. When both sides are golden in colour, serve very hot, garnished with lots of lemon wedges and parsley sprigs.

Parboiling it briefly lightens the rather overpowering flavour of this fast Baltic fish, ensuring that, this dish, though fried, is not the least bit heavy or indigestible.

CACCIUCCO

Fish soup

1.5kg / 3$^1/_4$ lb assorted fish (mullet, scorpion fish, sole, dogfish, mantis prawns, shellfish and what you will...)
125 ml/ 4 fl oz / $^1/_2$ cup white wine
500g / 1 lb 2 oz / 2$^1/_2$ cups puréed tomato
unsalted, stale bread
garlic
olive oil
parsley to taste

Servings: 4-6
Preparation time: 30′
Cooking time: 45′
Difficulty: ●●
Flavour: ●●●
Kcal (per serving): 503
Proteins (per serving): 47
Fats (per serving): 13
Nutritional value: ●●

When choosing the fish, do not turn your nose up at the cheaper and uglier varieties which, in fact, will surprise you with their excellent flavour. Clean and wash the fish (you could leave this chore up to the fishmonger). Brown the garlic in 4 tablespoons of oil in a large saucepan, add the powdered chilli pepper (the tip of a teaspoon) and the white wine. When the latter has evaporated, add the tomato paste and simmer for another 5 minutes over low heat. Add the fish, beginning with the variety needing the lengthiest cooking (dogfish), finishing up with that needing the least (mullet). Continue cooking over medium heat for a further quarter-hour, delicately moving the fish with the aid of a wooden spoon, so that the flavours of the sauce are absorbed well.
Toast some slices of bread and rub them liberally with garlic. Place one slice in each soup bowl, spoon over the "cacciucco", smothering the toast in the fish stock. Serve at once, with a sprinkling of parsley, if you wish.

This tasty fish soup, which, in deference to recent alimentary practice, I prefer to serve as a main course (or rather as a light luncheon dish) instead of as just the first course, is usually ascribed to the Livornese culinary tradition.
However, seeing that Livorno was founded by Florence, this exceptional recipe is, "tout court", officially relegated to Tuscan culinary traditions.

INZIMINO DI SEPPIE

Squid stew

1kg / 2 1/4 lb squid
2 bunches of swiss chard
2 cloves of garlic
125ml / 4 fl oz / 1/2 cup white wine
bunch of parsley
200g / 7 oz / 1 cup home-made tomato sauce
olive oil

Servings: 6
Preparation time: 30′
Cooking time: 1h ca
Difficulty: ●●
Flavour: ●●●
Kcal (per serving): 349
Proteins (per serving): 40
Fats (per serving): 14
Nutritional value: ●

Strip off the central midribs from the chard, rinse the leaves and cook in boiling water. Drain and squeeze the moisture out, putting to one side for the moment. Clean the squid (a chore that the fishmonger will happily undertake for you), removing the ink-sac and central rostrum. Slice the sac into rings and cut the tentacles into chunks. Fry the two cloves of garlic with 3 tablespoons of oil in a saucepan. When it colours, add the squid and white wine.
Put on the lid and simmer for 10 minutes over a low flame. Then add the chard (you can chop it up with a "mezzaluna" rocker knife), salt, pepper and tomato sauce. Cover the pan and simmer over low heat for about 40 minutes.
You may indeed ask ,"Why squid, when the traditional recipe calls for cuttlefish?" Because squid are more delicate and tender. But, should you wish to try it with cuttlefish, I will not be the least perturbed.

The splendid bay at Procchio, on the island of Elba.

About 1kg / $2^1/4$ lb octopus
1 stick of celery
1 carrot
2 bay leaves
5 black peppercorns
white wine
125ml / 4 fl oz / $^1/2$ cup each
white wine and red wine vinegar
thin-rinded lemon
parsley
olive oil

Servings: 4
Preparation time: 30'
Cooking time: 1h 30'+2h
Difficulty: ●●
Flavour: ●●
Kcal (per serving): 245
Proteins (per serving): 28
Fats (per serving): 13
Nutritional value: ●

POLPO MARINATO

Marinated octopus

Clean the octopus and place in a pan of cold water with the celery, roughly-chopped carrot, bay leaves, the white wine and peppercorns. Cover and bring to the boil, then lower the heat. With the lid still on, simmer for an hour and a half. Do not attempt to eat immediately it is cooked, but allow it to cool in its stock. This is the secret for making your octopus tasty and tender. Cut it into pieces and place in a bowl. Sprinkle with oil, the vinegar and some lemon juice, adding the zest, too, shredded and without any pith. Shake a little parsley over, but wait at least another hour before relishing this dish.

Bocca di Magra: the sea and the Apuan Alps.

OMELETTES

5

FRITTATA DI RICOTTA

Ricotta cheese omelette

200g / 7 oz ewe's milk ricotta cheese
50g / 2 oz / 1/4 cup grated Parmesan
6 eggs
1/2 white onion
2 ripe tomatoes
olive oil

Servings: 4
Preparation time: 20′+20′
Cooking time: 35′
Difficulty: ●●
Flavour: ●●
Kcal (per serving): 404
Proteins (per serving): 27
Fats (per serving): 30
Nutritional value: ●●

With a wooden spoon, work the ricotta (previously drained in cheesecloth) together with the Parmesan cheese in a bowl. Season with salt and pepper and leave to stand a while. Sauté the sliced onion with the chopped tomatoes in 2 tablespoons of oil for 10 minutes. Beat the eggs. Heat a non-stick pan, pour in a trickle of oil (the omelette will slip out more easily) and spoon over a ladle of the egg mixture. Cook the omelette slowly, pricking the surface several times and draw off the heat without ever turning it over. Make 3 more omelettes in this way, filling the centre with the cheese preparation. Roll each omelette up and place these rolls in the tomato sauce. Heat over a high flame for a few moments and serve the omelettes masked in sauce.

My grandmother used to recite "butter from the cow, cacio (a hard cheese) from the sheep, ricotta from the goat", in the times when the ingredients were precisely those. It is not easy to find ricotta from goats nowadays, in fact it is more likely to be made from pure sheep's milk. However, watch out in June and July, the lambing season, when it is hard to find ewe's milk.

FRITTATA DI CIPOLLE

Onion omelette

6 red-skinned onions
2 tablespoons of olive oil
4 eggs

Servings: 4
Preparation time: 10′
Cooking time: 20′
Difficulty: ●●
Flavour: ●●
Kcal (per serving): 253
Proteins (per serving): 15
Fats (per serving): 16
Nutritional value: ●

Slice the onions into rings and sauté in a frying pan until golden. Beat the eggs with salt and pepper. Pour into the pan, raising the heat a little. Allow to set on one side, toss the omelette over and brown on the other side.

This is excellent, either hot or cold. A delicious way of offering it, either as a complete light meal or as a starter, is to take some bread chunks and cubes of omelette (thicker and more solid) and pumpkin (in winter) or melon (in summer), impaling them alternately on skewers.

FRITTATA DI POMODORI VERDI

Green tomato omelette

2 green salad tomatoes
3 eggs
olive oil

Servings: 4
Preparation time: 20′
Cooking time: 20′
Difficulty: ●●
Flavour: ●●
Kcal (per serving): 203
Proteins (per serving): 9
Fats (per serving): 17
Nutritional value: ●

Rinse the tomatoes well and cut them into rounds horizontally, i.e. across their width. It is advisable to remove the seeds scrupulously, as well.
Coat the tomato slices with flour and deep fry in hot oil, turning them so that they are nicely browned on both sides.
When well-cooked (10 minutes will be needed for a good fry which is reasonably springy), place them in a baking dish and pour over the lightly-beaten eggs.
Put in a hot oven for about 5/7 minutes and serve the omelette very hot, but still a little runny in the centre (or else, if you like, leave the omelette in the oven a few moments more to cook right through and make the tomatoes nice and crisp).

FRITTATA DI FIORI DI ZUCCA

Courgette (zucchini) flower omelette

500g / 1 lb 2 oz courgette (zucchini) flowers
2 cloves of garlic
6 freshly-laid eggs
catmint
olive oil

Servings: 6	
Preparation time: 20′	
Cooking time: 20′	
Difficulty: ●●	
Flavour: ●●●	
Kcal (per serving): 287	
Proteins (per serving): 17	
Fats (per serving): 23	
Nutritional value: ●	

Clean the courgette flowers, leaving the pistils intact, and tear them into pieces. Put a little oil in a frying pan with a handful of catmint and the garlic and scald the flowers slightly (they must keep their bright yellow colour). Allow to cool and add the beaten egg. Fry everything in a barely-greased frying pan and make a soft, light omelette.

Although catmint plays an important role in my recipe, I can assure you that the success of the dish is guaranteed even without that extra touch. Alternatively, use a pinch of thyme (even if dried), but only a pinch!

6 small, tender globe artichokes
6 freshly-laid eggs
white flour
olive oil

Servings: 6	
Preparation time: 20′	
Cooking time: 20′	
Difficulty: ●●	
Flavour: ●●	
Kcal (per serving): 305	
Proteins (per serving): 16	
Fats (per serving): 21	
Nutritional value: ●	

TORTINO DI CARCIOFI ▸

Artichoke omelette

Clean the artichokes and remove the stems. Cut them into thickish wedges, dredge with flour and fry in an ovenproof dish. When they are golden on both sides, pour the beaten egg over and lightly season with salt and pepper. Now it depends on your taste; if you like the omelette cooked well and not "creamy", bake in a hot oven for a few minutes, otherwise, enjoy it as it is, not completely set, but (to my way of thinking) fresher and more appetising.

TORTINO ALLA FIORENTINA

Florentine omelette

Slice the courgettes into rounds and sauté until golden in 2 tablespoons of oil in a frying pan.
Turn them over to brown on both sides. Lightly beat the eggs, adding the milk, salt and pepper. When the vegetables are well-cooked (they must cook slowly for about a quarter-hour), throw in the beaten eggs. Let the omelette set on one side, then, helping yourself with the pan lid, turn it over to brown on the other side. Serve the omelette dusted with a pinch of marjoram.

This traditional Tuscan omelette is delicious especially in summer, when fresh courgettes can be used (those that "sing", or rather, make a cheerful sound, when rubbed against your hands). It also makes an excellent dish served cold the following day.

Aerial view of the Charterhouse of Florence.

300g / 11 oz small, fresh courgettes (zucchini)
5 whole eggs
60ml / 2 fl oz / 1/4 cup milk
pinch of marjoram
olive oil

Servings: 4
Preparation time: 15′
Cooking time: 30′
Difficulty: ●●
Flavour: ●●
Kcal (per serving): 271
Proteins (per serving): 15
Fats (per serving): 22
Nutritional value: ●

UOVA AL POMODORO

Tomato eggs

4 fresh eggs
2 very ripe tomatoes
basil
olive oil

Servings: 4
Preparation time: 10′
Cooking time: 15′
Difficulty: ●●
Flavour: ●●
Kcal (per serving): 265
Proteins (per serving): 14
Fats (per serving): 22
Nutritional value: ●

For 10 minutes, cook the tomatoes in 2 tablespoons of oil in a small frying pan. Season with salt and pepper, break in the eggs and mix, taking care not to break the yolks. Add yet another pinch of salt and pepper and keep over the heat until the whites have set. Serve nice and hot with sprigs of fresh basil.

VEGETABLE DISHES

6

ASPARAGI ALLA FIORENTINA

Asparagus, Florentine style

1kg / $2^1/4$ lb asparagus
80g / 3 oz / $^1/4$ cup plus 2 tbsp butter
4 eggs
grated Parmesan
freshly-ground pepper

Servings: 4
Preparation time: 15′
Cooking time: 30′
Difficulty: ●●
Flavour: ●●
Kcal (per serving): 194
Proteins (per serving): 19
Fats (per serving): 34
Nutritional value: ●●●

Trim the asparagus and scrape. Tie into bundles and place them carefully upright in a saucepan, pouring in enough cold water to cover the white part. Put on the lid and boil for a quarter-hour, without ever lifting the lid. Remove the vegetables from the pan and test their consistency; they must be cooked, but firm. Cut away the white part and place the green tips in a saucepan where you have melted a little butter. Sauté the asparagus over low heat for 5 minutes, turning them over with a wooden spoon. Dust liberally with Parmesan cheese, salt and pepper. Arrange the asparagus in a circle on a dish with the tips pointing inwards and serve with the eggs (one per person, fried separately) lying on the green tips.

BACCELLI STUFATI

Braised broad beans

2kg / $4^1/2$ lb fresh broad (fava) beans
1 white-skinned onion
4 red, ripe tomatoes
basil
olive oil

Servings: 6
Preparation time: 30′
Cooking time: 35′
Difficulty: ●●
Flavour: ●●●
Kcal (per serving): 646
Proteins (per serving): 42
Fats (per serving): 15
Nutritional value: ●●●

Hull the broad (fava) beans. Sauté the onion in 4 tablespoons of oil in a saucepan until translucent. Add the beans, the peeled tomatoes cut into pieces, the basil, salt and pepper. Cover and cook slowly for half-an-hour, stirring with a wooden spoon. At the end, add a dash of chilli pepper paste.

Partial view of the Piazza dei Miracoli in Pisa, with the Putto Fountain and the famous leaning Tower.

Cardi trippati

Braised cardoons

800g / 1³/4 lb cardoons
100g / 4 oz / ¹/2 cup butter
1 white-skinned onion
1 lemon
1 tablespoon white flour
grated Parmesan cheese

Servings: 6
Preparation time: 20′
Cooking time: 2h 10′
Difficulty: ●●
Flavour: ●
Kcal (per serving): 257
Proteins (per serving): 6
Fats (per serving): 28
Nutritional value: ●●●

Pick over the cardoons (they should be small or medium-sized, the larger ones being stringy with too much waste), removing the external midribs with their fibrous parts. Cut the tender stems into rather long chunks and cut the hearts of the cardoons up small. Dip in water acidulated with lemon juice, as cardoons tend to darken. Boil in lightly-salted water, adding a tablespoon of white flour to help maintain the cardoons' nice white colour. Cook slowly for two hours. Slice the onion finely and sauté in butter until it turns golden. Then add the cardoons and gently brown for 10 minutes. Transfer to a baking dish that retains the heat (they are only good if eaten hot) and serve with Parmesan cheese.

Fagioli all'olio

Beans in oil

500g / 1 lb 2 oz fresh cannellini or toscanello beans
olive oil
freshly-ground pepper
4 cloves of garlic
sprig of sage

Servings: 6
Preparation time: 6'
Cooking time: 45'
Difficulty: ●●
Flavour: ●●
Kcal (per serving): 370
Proteins (per serving): 22
Fats (per serving): 12
Nutritional value: ●●●

If you can, use fresh beans (if they are dried, soak them overnight in water, with the addition of a tablespoon of bicarbonate of soda or baking soda), hull them and boil in a little salted water, barely enough to cover, with garlic and sage.
Cook over a low heat for three quarters-of-an-hour, strictly keeping the pan covered.
Serve hot, dressed with plenty of high-quality extra-virgin olive oil and with a grinding of pepper over the top (if it is to your liking).

It is not really all that simple to cook the beans properly (if you have difficulty in tracking down the famous toscanello beans, do not despair because there are varieties of small, white beans which can easily substitute them). I remember my first experiences as a young, callow girl resulting in sad, mushy pulps or else with hard pieces wandering round the saucepan, with my mother and grandmother surveying it all with an interrogative air.
You see, the secret of this simple, plain dish lies wholly in the cooking, which must be slow and gentle, in a covered pan.
That is all. A plate of beans seasoned with good quality Tuscan oil, a nice slice of unsalted Tuscan bread and a good glass of wine - my husband says he would never tire of eating them! Try them in June in the Tuscan countryside, in the shade of a vine, and you will appreciate that here is the secret of our cuisine.

FAGIOLI ALL'UCCELLETTO

Beans with tomato sauce

500g / 1 lb 2 oz fresh cannellini beans (200g / 7 oz if dried)
3 cloves of garlic
sprig of sage
5 ripe tomatoes
olive oil
chilli pepper

Servings:	6
Preparation time:	10'
Cooking time:	1 h ca
Difficulty:	●●
Flavour:	●●●
Kcal (per serving):	335
Proteins (per serving):	14
Fats (per serving):	11
Nutritional value:	●●●

Boil the beans, adding a tablespoon of oil (if they are dried, soak them first for 2 hours), removing from the heat while they are still "al dente". In a casserole of terracotta (but steel will do), sauté the garlic and sage in 6 tablespoons of oil and add the peeled, roughly-chopped tomatoes. Reduce over medium heat for about 10 minutes, stirring with a wooden spoon. Add the beans with a little of their cooking water. Simmer over a low flame for a quarter-hour, add salt and pepper (or a little chilli pepper).

A classic of Tuscan tradition, it discloses a masterly fusion of flavours in its simplicity. The origin of the definition "all'uccelletto" remains shrouded in mystery, just like the names of so many other traditional dishes. The most likely conjecture is that it refers to the presence of sage, an essential ingredient when cooking little birds, in Italian "uccellini". Strangely enough, Artusi (the foremost Italian cookery expert) was a fore-runner in recommending their use as a light luncheon dish; "These beans go very well with boiled meats, if you do not wish to eat them on their own". He first adds the beans and then the tomatoes, but I go my own sweet way.

Fagioli nel fiasco

Beans in a flask

350g / 3/4 lb small dried haricot beans
sage leaves
cloves of garlic
olive oil
peppercorns

Servings: 4
Preparation time: 15′
Cooking time: 2-3h
Difficulty: ●●
Flavour: ●●
Kcal (per serving): 370
Proteins (per serving): 22
Fats (per serving): 12
Nutritional value: ●●●

Soak the dried beans for about an hour in slightly tepid water. Drain them and drop them one by one (it is worth the trouble!) into a Chianti flask devoid of its traditional straw covering, along with the sage and 2 cloves of garlic. Add cold water and olive oil until the flask is full to the neck. Bung it with a wad of cotton wool so that the contents do not spill out but excess steam can escape. If you have a fireplace, place the flask on a bed of ashes and embers so that it is partially covered. Too intense heat would cause the flask to explode, so do not put it too close to the roaring part of the fire. Make sure that the heat is always uniform.
If you do not have a wood fire, cook the beans by placing a rolled-up cloth on the bottom of a saucepan to form a kind of nest. Stand the flask on it upright and pour water into the pan so that the flask is almost completely covered. Bring to the boil and keep on the hob for 2 hours. Always remember to add hot water to the saucepan as it evaporates. "Fagioli al fiasco" are excellent hot or cold, seasoned, of course, with plenty of olive oil and freshly-ground pepper. They are delicious when served with fresh, thinly-sliced onions.

FAGIOLINI IN UMIDO

Ragout of runner beans

500g / 1 lb 2 oz runner beans
1 ripe tomato
125ml / 4 fl oz / 1/2 cup stock
1 onion
olive oil

Servings: 6
Preparation time: 15′
Cooking time: 35′
Difficulty: ●●
Flavour: ●●
Kcal (per serving): 154
Proteins (per serving): 3
Fats (per serving): 10
Nutritional value: ●●

Top, tail and string the runner beans. Rinse under the tap and place in a sieve. Meanwhile, slice the onion finely and sauté in a saucepan with 4 tablespoons of oil. When it has turned golden in colour, add the peeled and chopped tomato, the stock and the runner beans, adding a pinch of salt and pepper. Cover with the lid and cook over a low flame for half-an-hour. Relish this fragrant, appetising side-plate especially in the summer, the season which is sacred for runner beans (the long, tasty variety we call Sant'Anna, recommended for this recipe, gets its name because it ripens towards the end of July when the saint's name-day falls). This is excellent served on its own for a light luncheon.

FUNGHI FRITTI

Mushroom fritters

500g / 1 lb 2 oz porcini/cep mushrooms (*boletus edulis*)
2 eggs
100g / 4 oz / 2/3 cup plain flour
olive oil

Servings: 4-6
Preparation time: 20′
Cooking time: 20′
Difficulty: ●●
Flavour: ●●
Kcal (per serving): 414
Proteins (per serving): 12
Fats (per serving): 32
Nutritional value: ●●●

Some people only fry the caps, but I personally find that the stems of mushrooms (if they are unblemished, of course) are also truly excellent. Clean the mushrooms carefully, separating the stems, which you will scrape with the blade of a knife, and wiping the caps with a damp cloth to remove any grit. Cut up both caps and stems and place in a bowl with the eggs and flour. Blend with the other ingredients and fry in boiling oil, removing from the pan after a few minutes when they are crisp and golden, before they risk turning black and bitter. Eat them hot and crunchy. Some recipes omit the egg, but I would not because it gives the *boletus edulis* mushrooms a pleasant touch.

PISELLI ALLA FIORENTINA

Florentine peas

Having shelled and rinsed the peas, cook them in a saucepan with the oil, the garlic in its "jacket" (i.e. do not remove the skin from each clove) and all the parsley.
Douse the peas with a little cold water and cook them with the lid on for a good quarter-hour. Add the diced bacon.
Bring the peas to the boil once more, adding the sugar, salt and a little pepper.

1kg / 2 1/4 lb fresh garden peas
100g / 4 oz unsmoked fatty bacon
1 lemon
3 cloves of garlic
sprig of parsley
1 tsp granulated sugar
6 tablespoons olive oil

Servings: 6
Preparation time: 15′
Cooking time: 20′
Difficulty: ●●
Flavour: ●●
Kcal (per serving): 564
Proteins (per serving): 30
Fats (per serving): 39
Nutritional value: ●●●

SEDANI RIPIENI

Stuffed celery

1 large head of celery
About 100g / 4 oz each minced (ground) veal and pork, leg of lamb and chicken livers
50g / 2 oz each boiled ham and mortadella
2 whole eggs and 2 yolks
50g / 2 oz / 6 tbsp grated Parmesan
1/2 l / 1pt / 2 1/4 cups puréed tomato
125ml / 4 fl oz / 1/2 cup white wine
onion, carrot and celery
olive oil

Servings: 6
Preparation time: 20′
Cooking time: 35′
Difficulty: ●●
Flavour: ●●
Kcal (per serving): 537
Proteins (per serving): 28
Fats (per serving): 30
Nutritional value: ●●●

Choose the tenderest stalks, discarding the toughest ones and the leaves. Rinse and blanche for a few minutes in boiling water. Drain and place on a tea towel to dry. Mix the three types of meat with the chopped ham and mortadella in a bowl, adding the yolks and the grated Parmesan. Blend all the ingredients and stuff the celery, opening out and flattening the stalks. Close each stalk carefully, dip in flour and then into the beaten egg and fry in 6 tablespoons of oil in a saucepan over low heat for 20 minutes, stirring. In a separate pan, make a mirepoix and add the chopped chicken livers together with the white wine. Sauté for 10 minutes, then add the tomato purée. Place the stuffed celery stalks in this sauce, bring to the boil again and season with salt and pepper. Serve very hot.

DESSERTS, CAKES AND PASTRIES

7

500g / 1 lb 2oz/ $3^1/3$ cups plain flour
400g / 14 oz / 2 cups granulated sugar
250g / 9 oz / $2^1/2$ cups almonds
3 whole eggs and 2 egg yolks
1 beaten egg
1 tsp baking powder

Servings: 6
Preparation time: 30′
Cooking time: 1h
Difficulty: ●●●
Kcal (per serving): 1350
Proteins (per serving): 41
Fats (per serving): 46
Nutritional value: ●●●

Biscotti di Prato

Prato biscuits (cookies)

Thoroughly mix all the ingredients (with the exception of the beaten egg) and knead. If necessary, add a few drops of milk, bearing in mind that the dough must be smooth but not sticky.
Shape into two stick loaves 4 in wide and 12 in long, brush with the beaten egg and dust with sugar.
Place on a baking tray lined with greaseproof or baking paper and cook in a low oven for at least an hour.
When the surface is crisp and golden, remove from the oven and, using a wide-bladed knife, cut the loaves obliquely into biscuits 1/2 in thick while they are still hot.
Once cold, these biscuits can be kept for a long time in an air-tight container, so that they do not lose their fragrance.
It is traditional to serve them together with a glass of vinsanto, into which they are dunked.

BRUCIATE

Roast chestnuts

Make a slit in the skin (the Tuscans call it rather disturbingly "castrating") and place over a fierce heat in the special roasting pan with holes in the bottom, frequently turning the nuts over.
The fire really should be a log one, but, as not everyone possesses a fireplace, the kitchen hob will do.
When they are cooked and a little burnt (do not worry if the skins are somewhat charred) wrap them up in a length of woollen cloth and let them "stew" a little. Enjoy them while still scorching hot.

1kg / 2 1/4 lb chestnuts (preferably choice marrons)

Servings: 4-6
Preparation time: 15′
Cooking time: 20′
Difficulty: ●
Kcal (per serving): 378
Proteins (per serving): 7
Fats (per serving): 4
Nutritional value: ●●●

A tasty alternative is to soak them in a bowl of red vintage wine, once the nuts are cooked and peeled.

BRUTTI MA BUONI

Almond meringues

4 egg whites
30g / 1 oz / 1/3 cup almonds, peeled
30g / 1 oz / 1/3 cup hazelnuts, shelled
50g / 2 oz / 1/4 cup vanilla sugar
100g / 4 oz / 1/2 cup butter

Servings: 4
Preparation time: 20′
Cooking time: 30′
Difficulty: ●●
Kcal (per serving): 417
Proteins (per serving): 9
Fats (per serving): 36
Nutritional value: ●●●

Whisk the egg whites until fluffy, gradually adding the sugar (never add it all at once if you do not want the mixture to collapse).
Toast the almonds and hazelnuts briefly in the oven, then chop roughly. Slowly add the nuts to the meringue mixture. Spoon small quantities onto a greased baking tray. Bake in a pre-heated, very slow oven for half-an-hour until you get little, crisp "mounds". Leave to cool and ... tuck in!

CASTAGNACCIO

Chestnut cake

200g / 7 oz / 1 1/4 cups chestnut flour
125ml / 4 fl oz / 1/2 cup cold water
6 tbsp oil
rosemary
a handful each of pine-nuts and sultanas

Servings: 4
Preparation time: 15'+30'
Cooking time: 45'
Difficulty: ●●
Kcal (per serving): 338
Proteins (per serving): 5
Fats (per serving): 26
Nutritional value: ●●●

"Castagnaccio" must be of a nice brown colour with the top all wrinkled. The secret lies in the flour used; be cautious of flour on sale in October, because it is left over from the previous year. Genuine chestnut flour does not reach shop shelves before half-way through November, is mealy and sweet (indeed, the addition of sugar should not be necessary) and is good enough to eat raw.

Steep the sultanas in hot water. Pour the chestnut flour into a bowl where you have put 2 tablespoons of genuine olive oil. Gradually add the cold water, stirring with a whisk to obtain a pouring mixture without lumps. Set the mixture aside for at least half an hour and, in the meanwhile, oil a shallow rectangular cake tin.

Heat 3 tablespoons of oil in a small saucepan and throw in the rosemary leaves for a short moment to flavour it.

Pour the mixture into the cake tin, sprinkle the pine-nuts and the well-dried sultanas over the top and drizzle over the rosemary-flavoured oil too, together with the rest of the oil.

Bake in the oven at 220°C / 425°F / Gas Mark 7 for 30-40 minutes.

Cenci

Fried pastry twists

300g / 11 oz / 2 cups plain flour
50g / 2 oz / 1/4 cup butter
2 eggs
1 tbsp granulated sugar
1 tbsp Marsala
pinch of salt
200g / 7 oz / 1 cup vanilla sugar
olive oil

Servings: 4
Preparation time: 30'+1h
Cooking time: 20'
Difficulty: ●●
Kcal (per serving): 805
Proteins (per serving): 8
Fats (per serving): 38
Nutritional value: ●●●

Mound the flour up on a board and, in a hollow in the centre, place the butter (soft, not straight out of the refrigerator), the sugar, the eggs, a tablespoon of Marsala and a pinch of salt. Work the dough in your fingers until it is firm (add a little flour, if necessary). Cover and leave to "rest" for an hour in a dry place. Roll out the dough quite thinly and cut into strips about 2 inches by 4 (however, the size is up to you; it would appear that they are called "cenci" or "rags" precisely because they come in different shapes and sizes!). Deep fry in boiling oil. They are ready when they turn crisp and golden; be careful not to overcook and burn them. Drain and dust liberally with vanilla sugar.

These pastry twists are good to eat either boiling hot or cold. They are consumed both at Carnival time (when they are customary in Tuscany) and also in the height of summer, perhaps at a child's birthday party, seeing as they are not at all indigestible and are easy to make. Everyone makes his or her own slight modifications to the basic recipe or even to the shape (for example, some cooks tie the ribbons of dough before frying them or they clip the edges into fringes). Creativity is welcome, for the flavour of "cenci" is always appreciated.

FRITTELLE DI RISO

Rice fritters

500g / 1 lb 2 oz / 2 cups rice
1/2 l / 18 fl oz / 2 cups milk
200g / 7 oz / 1 1/3 cups muscatel raisins
1 orange and 1 lemon
500g / 1 lb 2 oz / 2 1/3 cups granulated sugar
1 liqueur glass of marsala
1 tbsp plain flour
3 whole eggs and 2 egg yolks
pinch of baking powder
olive oil

Servings: 4-6
Preparation time: 25′
Cooking time: 1h
Difficulty: ●●●
Kcal (per serving): 1695
Proteins (per serving): 35
Fats (per serving): 66
Nutritional value: ●●●

Put the rice in a saucepan with half a litre (1 pint / 2 1/4 cups) of cold water, the cold milk, the orange and the lemon, sliced. Cook for 20 minutes over low heat, stirring with a wooden spoon. Add 300g (11 oz / 1 1/2 cups) of sugar and continue cooking over gentle heat for another 20 minutes, still stirring. Before drawing off the heat, add the raisins and the Marsala. Allow to cool and remove the orange and lemon. Add the flour, whole eggs, yolks and the baking powder. Stir with a wooden spoon and deep fry, dropping spoonfuls of the mixture into the oil. The fritters must float on top (if they sink, raise the heat because the oil is obviously at too low a temperature). Allow to brown evenly all over, drain well and roll in plenty of fine sugar. Serve them hot.

According to tradition, rice fritters are prepared for St Joseph's Day on 19 March which used to be a holiday, but is now a day like any other. A pity! Even if we have been robbed of a holiday in the interests of productivity, we will certainly not give up the habit of these delicious little fritters, typical of Florentine cookery. I warn you that they seem easy to make, but that, on the contrary, a lot of care is needed to make them nice and golden and not soggy with oil, as are so many of those you find in the shops.

120g / 4 oz / 1 cup plain flour
20g / 3/4 oz / 2 tbsp bitter cocoa powder
2 egg whites
1 orange
20g / 3/4 oz / 2 tbsp bitter cocoa powder
150g / 5 oz / 1 cup + 2 tbsp icing (confectioners') sugar

Servings: 4
Preparation time: 20'
Cooking time: 10'
Difficulty: ●●
Kcal (per serving): 291
Proteins (per serving): 8
Fats (per serving): 2
Nutritional value: ●●●

QUARESIMALI

Lenten Biscuits

Grate the orange peel (it should not be too coarse) and place all the ingredients in a bowl where you will blend them thoroughly, by giving a good, lengthy beating with a wooden spoon.
A thick cream will be the end result. Spoon a portion into a pastry bag with a smooth nozzle and squeeze the mixture onto a lightly-buttered baking tray, forming the letters of the alphabet.
Do not write them too big (1 1/2 in - 2 in high at the most) and space them out well, because they need room to spread in the cooking. Bake in a slow oven for at least 10 minutes.

If your efforts with a pastry bag are not entirely satisfactory, you can easily get hold of little letter-shaped moulds which will provide you with more aesthetically acceptable "quaresimali".

All things considered, the originality of the recipe, which is exceedingly simple, lies in the shape of the biscuits, so they might as well be done properly.

The name of this biscuit tells us when they were traditionally made. At one time, there was not a pastry-shop or baker's here in Florence which, during Lent, did not exhibit conspicuous heaps of the biscuits, which sold like ... hotcakes! Understandably so, because the abstemious period following the Carnival festival offers the palate scarce gratification. Now that they have rather gone out of fashion, make them yourselves, for the children's birthdays, perhaps. They will have great fun - so do I - making up words from the brown letters, only to crunch them up happily!

SALAME DI CIOCCOLATA

Chocolate sausage

300g / 11 oz biscuits (not made with eggs)
150g / 5 oz / $^{3}/_{4}$ cup granulated sugar
150g / 5 oz / $^{3}/_{4}$ cup butter
50g / 2 oz / $^{1}/_{2}$ cup pine nuts
2 tbsp bitter cocoa
1 liqueur glass of sweet marsala

Servings: 4-6
Preparation time: 30′+2h
Difficulty: ●●
Kcal (per serving): 902
Proteins (per serving): 8
Fats (per serving): 51
Nutritional value: ●●●

Finely crumble the biscuits into a bowl and add the butter (melted, but not hot), sugar and cocoa. Blend the mixture with a spoon and gradually add the Marsala. Continue working with your hands and add the coarsely-chopped pine-nuts. Form the mixture into an elongated sausage shape and place in the refrigerator, well-wrapped in aluminium foil. When it is time to serve it, cut into slices half-an-inch thick and offer them on a round plate.

If you like, you could complement this with a light custard for spreading on top. To make it, you need 2 egg yolks, beaten in a bowl with 50g / 2 oz / $^{1}/_{4}$ cup of granulated sugar. Add 20 g / $^{3}/_{4}$ oz / 3 tbsp flour and $^{1}/_{2}$l / 18 fl oz / 2$^{1}/_{4}$ cups milk at room temperature. First whisk well to blend off the heat, then put over very low heat, drawing it off as it bubbles at the sides.

The famous Carnival parade at Viareggio, with the huge allegorical floats.

SCHIACCIATA ALLA FIORENTINA

Florentine flat cake

500g / 1 lb 2 oz / $3^1/3$ cups plain flour
150g / 5 oz / $^3/4$ cup lard
20g / $^3/4$ oz fresh yeast or 3 tsp active dry yeast
150g / 5 oz / $^3/4$ cup granulated sugar
4 egg yolks
1 orange
salt, vanilla sugar

Servings: 4-6
Tempo di prep.: 30′+1h+2h
Cooking time: 30′
Difficulty: ●●
Kcal (per serving): 1127
Proteins (per serving): 27
Fats (per serving): 50
Nutritional value: ●●●

Dissolve the yeast in water which is barely warm and add to the flour in a bowl, working it in until you get a firm dough (that comes away easily from the sides of the bowl). Cover and leave in a dry place to prove for an hour. When doubled in size, mix in the egg yolks, sugar, $^2/3$ of the lard, a pinch of salt and the finely-grated orange peel, working it all in your fingers to blend the ingredients thoroughly. With the lard left over, grease a deep, rectangular cake tin and press the dough in, making sure that it is of even thickness all over (about an inch). Be careful here, because herein lies the secret of success. Leave it for 2 hours to rise again. Bake in a hot oven for half-an-hour. Turn out and dust with vanilla sugar.

SCHIACCIATA CON L'UVA

Grape dough cake

500g / 1 lb 2 oz bread dough
1kg / 2 1/4 lb wine grapes
8 tbsp granulated sugar
rosemary
2 tbsp olive oil

Servings: 6	
Preparation time: 15'+40'	
Cooking time: 30'	
Difficulty: ●●	
Kcal (per serving): 620	
Proteins (per serving): 13	
Fats (per serving): 6	
Nutritional value: ●●●	

Sprinkle over 8 tablespoons of red wine before baking. Besides imparting flavour, it will lend an attractive dark red colour. I advise using small, juicy black wine grapes for this cake, typically baked in the period between the end of summer and the beginning of autumn.

Knead the dough (see the recipe below), rendered more pliable with the addition of a tablespoon of oil, for five minutes. Grease a deep, rectangular cake tin and spread half of the dough on the bottom. Scatter over two thirds of the grapes, pressing them down and dusting with 3 tablespoons of sugar. Cover with the remaining dough, knocking it up well against the sides of the tin. Strew the remaining grapes on top, pushing down, and dredge with the remaining sugar. Sprinkle over a few rosemary needles and a little olive oil. Leave for 40 minutes and bake in a hot oven for half-an-hour, until a nice, golden crust has formed.

To make the dough, dissolve the yeast in a little warm water and add to the flour and oil in a bowl. Blend in and leave to rest for an hour in a dry place under the cover of a cloth.

At this point, the dough is ready for use in bread, pizzas or "focacce", but also in pasta, meat, fish and vegetable dishes where a crust is required, as well as in quiches that would go down a treat in the Lorraine.

ZUCCOTTO

Florentine cream gateau

To make the sponge base, whisk the eggs and sugar at length until the mixture is light and fluffy and can "write", i.e. a thread of the egg falling back into the bowl from the whisk will float for a moment. Should it immediately sink in, then the eggs are not sufficiently whisked. You will need about a quarter-hour, but do not rush the operation or the cake will come out barely risen and rubbery. Add the flour, grated lemon zest and a pinch of salt. Pour into the buttered and floured cake tin and bake for half-an-hour in a pre-heated, hot oven. Allow to cool before turning out, or the sponge will crumble. Whip the cream with the icing (confectioner's) sugar and chill. Prepare a dense chocolate sauce: put the butter, cocoa, sugar and about 4 tablespoons of water in a small saucepan, simmering for 5 minutes. Allow to cool, frequently stirring so that a skin does not form on the surface. When it is cold, add a third to the whipped cream and replace in the refrigerator. Mix the cubed candied peel and the roughly-grated chocolate with the rest of the whipped cream and allow this, too, to cool in the refrigerator. Cut the sponge cake into rectangular slices, brush well with vinsanto and use to line the calotte-shaped mould (which looks precisely like a cardinal's zucchetto). Pour the chocolate cream into the mould and fill up with the cream containing the candied peel. Cover with a disc of sponge cake steeped in vinsanto, pressing it down with your hands. Chill the gateau in the refrigerator (not in the freezer) for 4-5 hours.

4 eggs
150g / 5 oz / $^{3}/_{4}$ cup granulated sugar
150g / 5 oz / 1 cup plain flour
lemon zest
$^{1}/_{2}$ l / 18 fl oz / $2^{1}/_{4}$ cups cream
100g / 4 oz plain (semi-sweet) chocolate
100g / 4 oz / $^{1}/_{2}$ cup mixed candied fruit
50g / 2 oz / 6 tbsp icing (confectioner's) sugar
cocoa
20g / $^{3}/_{4}$ oz / $1^{1}/_{2}$ tbsp butter
sweet vinsanto (or sherry)

Servings: 4
Preparation time: 50'+5h
Cooking time: 40'
Difficulty: ●●●
Kcal (per serving): 1394
Proteins (per serving): 11
Fats (per serving): 95
Nutritional value: ●●●

TORTA "AI 7 CUCCHIAI"

"7-spoon" cake

400g / 14 oz / $3^2/_3$ cups plain flour
7 tbsp olive oil
7 tbsp granulated sugar
7 tbsp milk
3 eggs
pinch of baking powder
1 orange
knob of butter

Servings: 4 -6
Preparation time: 20′
Cooking time: 45′
Difficulty: ●●
Kcal (per serving): 433
Proteins (per serving): 11
Fats (per serving): 11
Nutritional value: ●●●

In a bowl, whisk together the oil, sugar and milk, gradually adding the eggs and the grated orange zest. Then, still whisking, sprinkle in the flour and finally the baking powder. Lightly butter and flour a deep, round cake tin. Bake the cake for three quarters-of-an-hour in a moderate oven and test it is cooked by inserting a toothpick or skewer into the cake, which should come out dry. Only at that point will the cake be ready.
Remove from the oven and leave to stand for a few minutes before turning it out onto a plate.

This makes an ideal cake base for fillings (e.g. with confectioner's custard, or with a sumptuous fig jam, as in the illustration).
Or, if sliced, it provides an ideal base for the preparation of Florentine Trifle.
If you wish to obtain a still softer cake, increase the quantity of olive oil by 1 or 2 table-spoons - "ça va sans dire" that it will of course be "extravergine".

ZUPPA DOLCE FIORENTINA

Trifle

1 "7-spoon cake" (please see the relative recipe)

the confectioner's custard:
2 eggs, separated
1/2 l / 18 fl oz / 2 1/4 cups milk
50g / 2 oz / 1/3 cup plain flour
lemon zest, grated
50g / 2 oz / 1/4 cup granulated sugar

the chocolate sauce:
50g / 2 oz / 1/2 cup bitter cocoa
30g / 1 oz / 3 tbsp plain flour
1/2 l / 18 fl oz / 2 1/4 cups milk
80g / 3 oz / 6 1/2 tbsp granulated sugar
knob of butter
a glass sweet marsala

Servings: 4
Preparation time: 20'+2h
Cooking time: 40' ca
Difficulty: ●●
Kcal (per serving): 654
Proteins (per serving): 19
Fats (per serving): 22
Nutritional value: ●●●

Make the confectioner's custard by whisking the egg yolks with the sugar and sprinkling in the flour and the milk. Bring to simmering point over a low flame, stirring continuously. Draw off the heat and dust with caster (powdered) sugar so that a skin does not form on the surface. The chocolate sauce is made by putting the cocoa, sugar and flour into another saucepan, all thinned down with the milk. Work everything in together well before placing over the heat. Cook very, very gently for about a quarter-hour. Lastly, add the butter and leave to cool.
Take a deep (preferably glass) dish and line it with inch-thick slices of the "7-Spoon" cake. Brush with Marsala. Pour a little custard into the bottom, cover with one or two slices of cake steeped in Marsala, then some chocolate sauce and so on until the dish is filled up. Place in the refrigerator and serve in ice-cream bowls (because it looks and tastes like an ice-cream cake) after two hours.

Some substitute coffee for Marsala, but I find the flavour too definite to blend well with the confectioner's custard and the chocolate sauce and at the same time "respect" their virtues.
The outcome may indeed be a trifle, but the flavour which prevails (overbearingly) is of coffee!